THE KINGDOM COACH
Remedial Training

MONICA A. ROBERTSON, PH.D.

Copyright © 2014 by Monica A. Robertson, Ph.D.

The Kingdom Coach
Remedial Training
by Monica A. Robertson, Ph.D.

Printed in the United States of America

ISBN 9781498412032

All rights reserved solely by the author. The author guarantees all contents are original and do not infringe upon the legal rights of any other person or work. No part of this book may be reproduced in any form without the permission of the author. The views expressed in this book are not necessarily those of the publisher.

Scripture.quotations taken from the Holy Bible, New International Version (NIV). Copyright © 1973, 1978, 1984, 2011 by Biblica, Inc.™. Used by permission. All rights reserved.

Scripture.quotations taken from the King James Version (KJV) – public domain

Scripture.quotations taken from the New Living Translation. Copyright ©1996, 2004, 2007 by Tyndale House Foundation. Used by permission of Tyndale House Publishers, Inc.

Scripture.quotations taken from the English Standard Version (ESV). Copyright © 2001 by Crossway, a publishing ministry of Good News Publishers. Used by permission. All rights reserved.

It is the writer's style to capitalize certain pronouns in Scripture that refer to the Father, Son, or the Holy Spirit. Take note that the name satan and other related names are not capitalized. The author chooses not to acknowledge him, even to the point of violating grammatical rules.

The internet addresses listed in the notes section were accurate at the time of publication. The inclusion of a Web site does not indicate an endorsement by the author, and the author does not guarantee the accuracy of all the information presented at these sites.

www.xulonpress.com

DEDICATION

My Coach

I want to dedicate this series to You first and foremost as You are the reason I can write these stories in a redemptive way. Your guidance and wisdom have helped me through years of training, eight years of education, and designing a business. Your partnership makes me look better than I could truly ever achieve on my own.

My husband and daughter

Thank you both for your love. God gave us the grace to grow together and I am grateful for the open communication we shared in tough times and the many moments of laughter in good times. I am so proud to be in this family with you. Honey, you are still the love of my life. Abbey, you are a joy to my soul and I am so proud of the wife and business woman you have become. You have both been so encouraging in the pursuit of my dreams these last couple of years.

Mom and Dad

I want to lovingly dedicate this first book in *The Kingdom Coach* series to you. Your humility and transparency allowed me to write this first book with confidence and peace. In spite of the struggles we all faced, your commitment to helping others find safety and to grow has always made an impression on my life. The Lord redeemed my season at home. He used it to train me and bless me. I feel closer to you both as together we have relived these stories and corroborated the facts for this book. You are absolutely the most generous people I have ever known.

Amy Ford

Thank you for your patience while editing this book. You are a great partner in ministry and a valuable resource in my life. You made this process easier and the book more enjoyable to read. I appreciate your friendship, knowledge, and wisdom. I am thankful for your involvement in what writing this book accomplished in me.

The brave souls who follow me on this journey

This book is a story of triumph for us all! It is book one in a series of Kingdom coaching principles. May the content inspire you to walk closer with the Holy Spirit. May you find any peace you have yet to attain and take the necessary steps to go one level deeper with Christ, one step higher in your freedom, and one step closer to the fulfillment of your destiny.

CONTENTS

Introduction ix

Chapter One	Do We Need Help?.................	17
Chapter Two	This is My Story	30
Chapter Three	Freedom from Pride & Presumption.....	72
Chapter Four	From Religion to Relationship	93
Chapter Five	Freedom from Biblical Illiteracy	121
Chapter Six	Freedom from Generational Sin.......	153
Chapter Seven	Freedom of Forgiveness.............	173
Chapter Eight	Invitation to the High Places.........	203

Appendix 215
Bibliography................................ 219

"Blessed be the God and Father of our Lord Jesus Christ, the Father of mercies and God of all comfort, who comforts us in all our affliction, so that we may be able to comfort those who are in any affliction, with the comfort with which we ourselves are comforted by God"

2 Corinthians 1:3-4

INTRODUCTION

"He lifted me out of the pit of despair, out of the mud and the mire. He set my feet on solid ground and steadied me as I walked along. He has given me a new song to sing, a hymn of praise to our God. Many will see what he has done and be amazed. They will put their trust in the LORD" (Psalm 40:2-3).

Compassion is a very important virtue. In fact, in all major religions, compassion is ranked as the highest virtue.[1] When you have walked a mile or two in another man's shoes, you have more patience with where he is going and what it will take to arrive at his destination. The Latin root of the word compassion means "co-suffering."[2] Having compassion is feeling deep care and concern for someone else's needs or struggles. Compassion possesses a desire to help people being patient with their progress, forgiving of their mistakes, and showing empathy to the burdens that can impede their progress. Healthy compassion is a desire to help others without becoming the source of their breakthrough, but understanding that only God can supply the grace and power necessary for such a victory. Compassion is one of the attributes that makes a great coach, and coaching is something I have loved for many years.

Before my compassion was in full bloom, I lived a challenging life, full of trials, disappointments, pain, and fear. I lived for years in what seemed like a valley surrounded by mountains, unequipped and lacking strength to climb even one passage that might lead to a good future. Dark forces stood guard all around the base of those mountains. Even thoughts and dreams about making the ascent were opposed by discouragement and futility. If I could break through the ranks of my enemy, would I make it up the mountain? Would they pursue me? What was on the other side? Could I survive there?

One day, to comfort myself, I began to sing. With eyes closed, I suddenly felt a new presence in the valley. It was then that I noticed Someone else standing at the base of the mountain. He was familiar to me. We had briefly met before, but He was so quiet that the noise of my enemy had caused me to forget that He was there. I supposed He had never left. It was as if He had been waiting on me to acknowledge Him. He made Himself available to me, but His approach was to put the burden of initiative on me to respond to His availability. That is what made Him such a great Coach. His presence gave me the hope that, just maybe, I could make it past the guards and up the mountain.

When I approached Him at the base of the mountain, I realized that the dark forces would still oppose my ascent. The Coach waited and He watched, but He did not force the guardians to allow me to pass. Was He not able? I did not know what to do and He did not offer. So we camped out at the base of the mountain.

I decided that since we were just camping, I would make the effort to get to know Him better. I discovered that He was very comfortable to be around and, surprisingly easy to engage in conversation. Through the course of our conversations, I finally became comfortable enough to ask about why I could not make the ascent. Perhaps it was fear of not being strong enough or the shame of being in the valley so long that caused me to avoid the question until then. Not that either one of those thoughts were true, but they felt true to me.

Introduction

I discovered that this Coach was not just a great Coach: He was also a great Counselor. While coaching is about discovery, counseling is about uncovering roadblocks and recovering from painful experiences that are buried within; both of which keep us reacting to life instead of responding to possibilities and opportunities. The Coach helped me to see why I was being opposed and how to resolve the problem. He helped me see that I was as afraid of making the climb, and the other side of that mountain, as I was about getting through the dark forces. He showed me how to overcome the opposition: where to obtain the weaponry, how to use it, and how soon I could get started! I was amazed at this wonderful Companion, who would spend time with a nobody, stuck in a valley of despair like me.

I did exactly as He said. Together we faced the opposition and broke through. Once we started ascending, I must admit, it seemed as if we took the longer route up the mountain. I was surprised that we battled more opposition on the way to the top, but as long as I followed the Coach, we kept breaking through the ranks.

When we finally reached the top, I was exhausted and stunned. The view was literally breathtaking and a bit daunting! For as much as I wanted to get to what was over that mountain, I suddenly froze. That was when He said, "You've made it this far. Why not keep going?"

I said, "Are You going with me?"

Then He said, "I will never leave you. I will never even turn my heart away from you. Besides, there are also others available to you on this journey. You will have all the help you need."

Mere words could not express what I felt in that moment. I sank to my knees, and with tears streaming down my face (like they are as I am writing), I sobbed as one long journey ended, and the first step of the next one waited before me.

Then I said, "Hey, can you teach me how to do what You do?"

As we walked, He said, "I already have."

Today, the Kingdom Coach is my business-ministry partner. You might know Him as the Holy Spirit, and He is amazing. The work He does and the roles He fills in my life and the lives of others is the continuous thread that you will read throughout *The Kingdom Coach* book series.

I am so thankful that I met the Coach. I needed Him so badly because, as the saying goes, "Everyone battles his demons." For many years, I was absolutely convinced that, I was battling mine alone.

What is all the talk about inner demons?

This year, I have noticed more talk than usual about battling inner demons. I have heard it spoken of in movies and in television series. This summer, after one of America's comedy legends tragically ended his life, I heard it in the news and in a flurry of Hollywood interviews. I have read about it in blogs. This phrase, "Battling inner demons" has been used in a variety of ways, and depending on who is talking, it can have several meanings.

For the eclectic crowd, it defines anyone's personal struggle with everything from physical pain to addiction and depression. For the scientific/philosophic community and their adherents, this phrase might refer to what Carl Jung called the darker side of man's personality. "'The shadow,' wrote Jung (1963), is 'that hidden, repressed, for the most part inferior and guilt-laden personality whose ultimate ramifications reach back into the realm of our animal ancestors and so comprise the whole historical aspect of the unconscious' (cited in Diamond, p. 96)."[3] Last but certainly not least, biblical believers use this phrase to describe the activity of actual demons: fallen celestial beings spoken of in the Bible. This latter belief is the foundation upon which *The Kingdom Coach* series is written.

We are all born in a war, and we are born for war (1 Timothy 6:12). Since the fall of man, there has been a battle raging for the souls of men. Satan, God's enemy, and man's adversary, has been contending for every human heart throughout history. From the day each of us is born, we are brought forth with a God-inspired plan already written for each of our lives (Psalm 139:16). We are also born in sin, and with a bounty on our heads (Psalm 51:5, Ephesians 2:1-4, John 10:10). As Jesus mentioned in the parable of the sower (Matthew 13, Luke 8, Mark 4), even after we hear the truth about the gospel, those precious seeds of truth have various degrees of vulnerability to the enemy, persecution, the cares of life, or the deceitfulness of wealth.

As a small child, God saw me on the battlefield. I was young and vulnerable, but He lovingly gave me this Coach: One who was there long before I realized, and One who has never left my side to this day. I now know that it was He who comforted me in childhood. He led me out of darkness. He carried me through many storms. He led me up the long path that prepared me for my destiny. Today, my job includes one of the ultimate purposes for which the Lord Himself came to earth: to destroy the work of the enemy (1 John 3:8) and to minister reconciliation to the lost and the broken.

Psalm 115:16 says, "The highest heavens belong to the Lord, but the earth He has given to the sons of men." In light of this reality, the question that begs an answer is this: How then should we live? Jesus Christ, through the Coach, answered this question for me in a lengthy illustrated sermon, one that encompasses my life from the beginning until now. The clash of activity between these dark forces and the Kingdom of Heaven has been impressed upon my struggle to freedom, my years of training and education, my calling and, no doubt, my ultimate destiny.

I asked the Coach once, "Why am I still here? Why did God not take me home?" His answer came on January 24, 1997: "I allowed you to become acquainted with death so that I could teach you how to live, and so you would go and teach others the same."

Through remedial, basic, and advanced level training, the Coach walked me through the steps to redeem my past. He led me into a deeper relationship with the Father, resulting in healing for my spirit, soul, and body. He used my own experiences to help me understand the biblical principles of spiritual warfare. Finally, He walked me through painful tests that forced my character to mature, making me into a stronger servant leader. He led me into my destiny: to teach and to counsel people who are seeking the truth that brings freedom from the past, peace for the present, and hope for the future.

The Kingdom Coach is a series of books of instruction within the setting of a true story. My prayer is that through my story, combined with truths and tools God has given me as a counselor, you will gain a better understanding of how we are all born into a battle for the destiny God planned for each of us (Romans 5:8, Ephesians 2:10) and the world in which we live (John 3:16, Ephesians 1:10). My hope is that *The Kingdom Coach* series will be inspirational for those of you who desire to initiate a deeper walk with the Lord, to identify and remove roadblocks, to mature in spiritual discipline, and to find the pathway to your destiny.

What is Remedial Training?

While some families do intentionally train their children for life, these families are the exception rather than the rule. It is not uncommon for children to grow up with limited knowledge in certain areas like finances, sexuality, communication, and self-discipline, or to leave home without necessary life skills such as balancing a checkbook, creating a budget, managing a home, finding a good job, or maintaining a car.

Remedial means, "intended to correct or improve one's skill in a specified area or to treat and cure something that is diseased."[4] Many people are in need of remedial help somewhere along the road of life. Not having it can result in incredible frustration, low self-worth, and tension in inter-personal relationships. This brokenness can lead to the difficult and often painful choice to seek help.

Seeking help is a humbling endeavor. Choosing help is often the road less traveled. But to those who desire wisdom in lieu of stumbling forward in weakness, it is liberating and an on-ramp to the highway of success in the pursuit of one's life goals. Finding help is a sign of wisdom, not weakness.

INTRODUCTION

PERSONAL APPLICATION

1. Who is the Kingdom Coach? _____
2. Do you currently enjoy a relationship with Him? Yes No
3. What other role does He play besides being a coach?

_____

4. Besides the examples already mentioned—finances, sexuality, communication, and self-discipline—can you think of some other areas of limited knowledge a person can have leaving home? If you had any, what were they (or what are they)?

_____

_____

4. What is the definition of the word "remedial"?

_____

5. Have you ever needed remedial help? How did it make you feel when you realized you needed it?

_____

_____

6. Do you agree with the statement, "Finding help is a sign of wisdom, not weakness?"   Yes   No

7. If you got the help you needed, how did you feel after you completed the process?

_____

_____

8. If you did not go after the help you needed, or if you have recently recognized the need for help but have not taken a step towards getting it, where might you look for advice in your circle of relationships?

_____

_____

_____

9. Read Titus 2:1-8. Who do these verses suggest someone can go to for additional knowledge or life skills?

_____

_____

10. If you have a remedial need in an area of your life, perhaps there are small groups in your local church or a class offered through a local non-profit in your area. You might want to consider a life coach or a counselor. If you need help and you are ready to pursue help, write down a few ideas you might consider.

_____

_____

11. How can prayer help? Read Jeremiah 33:3.

_____

_____

_____

Chapter One

DO WE NEED HELP?

"But the Helper, the Holy Spirit, whom the Father will send in my name, He will teach you all things, and bring to your remembrance all that I said to you" (John 14:26).

I have met some people who were raised in a home where they felt loved and protected. They found Christ early in life. They were taught the Scriptures and they saw a model of morality. Even these people, as adults, are greatly challenged and tempted by the culture in which we live. The truth is that we all need the help, guidance, and the power of the Holy Spirit to help us make wise choices about where to draw boundaries with ourselves and our children.

Speaking with numerous people throughout the years of being a pastor's wife and a counselor, I believe that most enter adulthood needing help. It is because satan, our adversary, is watching to see where he might oppose each of us on our journey. But he does not wait until we are grown to attack us. So many people, although they are born again, and many for years, still struggle with beliefs that are rooted in childhood events, from as simple as a misunderstanding to as severe as abuse.

How powerful is the past?

In Romans 8:38-39, the Apostle Paul states, "For I am sure that neither death nor life, nor angels nor rulers, nor things present nor things to come, nor powers, nor height nor depth, nor anything else in all creation, will be able to separate us from the love of God in Christ Jesus our Lord." I agree. In all of my suffering, God was always standing near, and as I look back, I realize He loved me even when I was not acknowledging Him. His love was always available for me, but for a long time I could not receive it. I find it interesting that Paul mentions that nothing in the present or the future can separate us from God's love, but he does not mention the past. Sometimes the past can keep you from receiving God's love. What if you did not feel loved by your parents? What if you did not receive Christ in early childhood? What if you feel like you have never heard His voice? Of course, if you are saved, you have heard Him at least once. If these statements are true, then it is entirely possible that you could struggle with believing what God says about you or what He says about Himself because of the beliefs that are still in your heart from the past.

Regardless of what life was like in our past, we need to acknowledge the Coach, as it is He who gives us the continual sense of God's presence so that as we fellowship with Him, we can resolve any pain from the past. Whatever it takes, we must pursue Him until we are free from all that hinders us from enjoying Him and find the destiny that He prepared in advance for us (Ephesians 2:10).

Unresolved issues of the past can be discouraging. Discouragement held too long can cause us to harden our hearts against the truth and the promises of God's Word. We think God is being unfaithful, when in reality; we have refused to surrender something to Him and thus we are yielding to sin (James 4:17) and unbelief. We want Him to move when, in fact, He already has by allowing His Son to be crucified. We are the ones who are unwilling to move. He has already given us many promises of healing to appropriate into our own life circumstances through prayers and actions of faith.

The writer of Hebrews 3:7-8 states, "Therefore, as the Holy Spirit says, '**Today**, if you hear his voice, do not harden your hearts as in the rebellion, on the day of testing in the wilderness..." In other words, if God's Word tells you that you are loved, believe it. If God, in His Word, promises deliverance, believe Him. If the Holy Spirit speaks an encouraging word concerning your circumstances, whether straight to your heart, or through a person using the gift of prophecy, come into agreement with Him. Do not let your circumstances convince you to doubt God, like those who fell dead in the wilderness because they could not believe God could give them the land of their inheritance. Repent to God for unbelief. Then, renounce any agreement you have made with a spirit of unbelief and stretch out your faith, asking God for a turn in your circumstances. He is not moved by pity in regard to the needs of mankind, but by faith (Hebrews 11:6). He will act when we ask in faith with correct heart motives. (James 4:2). Hear God's voice and believe Him TODAY. Surrender your pain to Him and receive His comfort. If you do, His love will protect you from the overwhelming fear of your circumstances every day and into the future as well.

Some people feel so wounded and betrayed, on so many levels, that it is difficult for them to resolve the resulting pain and mistrust. They must pursue fellowship with God in childlike faith, through prayer and through a saturation of His Word. The Word of God is sharp and powerful enough to cut into these areas of their soul (Hebrews 4:12), enabling them to trust Him enough to surrender pain, lest they fall prey to a spirit of unbelief.

Hebrews 3:12-13 warns us stating,

> Take care, brothers, lest there be in any of you an evil, unbelieving heart, leading you to fall away from the living God. But exhort one another every day, as long

as it is called "today," that none of you may be hardened by the deceitfulness of sin.

Gill's Exposition of the Entire Bible says of this verse,

"...there is in every man, whether a profane sinner, or an hypocritical professor, an evil heart, and an unbelieving one; and there is unbelief in regenerate persons, which when cherished and encouraged by them is a great evil, and should be avoided; and this sin is aggravated by the many instances of God's grace, and by the many declarations of it, and by the exceeding great and precious promises God has made, and by the great discoveries of his love to their souls in times past: and this sin, when it gets ahead, has a very great influence on the heart, to make it evil; and unbelief was the first sin of man, at least it very early appeared; it is the mother sin, and puts persons upon every sin; it defiles the conscience, hardens the heart, renders the word unprofitable, unfit for duty and makes men unstable..."[1]

As you will see from my story, it took quite a while for me to trust God enough to surrender my pain. While I did not renounce my faith, I certainly did not pursue God much more than talking to Him. I did not pursue Him through the Word of God for quite some time, causing me to carry my pain too long, hurting my relationships in the process, and making it harder to break through when I finally surrendered. If this is your situation, as you continue to read, I encourage you to work through the application questions at the end of each chapter. It is always the right time to do what it right. It is not too late for you. There are many Christians carrying unnecessary pain today, and many who are struggling with their faith as a result. If you are one of them, consider making a choice to use this book as an aid to help you begin to lay aside this weight in your life.

Renewing our minds

Over the years, I have spoken with many middle aged people who were still saying, "What am I going to be when I grow up? Even if I figure out what that is, how will I ever achieve it with all that seems to hold me back?" I have to admit myself that I would not have discovered what I was supposed to do with my life or achieved it without the help of the Holy Spirit.
Romans 12:2, in the New International Version, states,

Do not conform to the pattern of this world, but be transformed by the renewing of your mind. Then you will be able to test and approve what God's will is—his good, pleasing and perfect will.

Matthew Henry's Concise Commentary says of this verse,

The work of the Holy Ghost first begins in the understanding, and is carried on to the will, affections, and conversation, till there is a change of the whole man into the likeness of God, in knowledge, righteousness, and true holiness. Thus, to be godly, is to give up ourselves to God.[2]

Sometimes, as in my case, people lack discipleship. They have simply not been diligent about knowing Christ through the Scriptures, through conversational prayer, and so on. Other times, they are so entrenched in the concrete of their past beliefs that they need an experience with God to overcome those beliefs and renew their minds to the truth.

When people come to me for counseling, no matter what they want to accomplish in counseling, I try to assess what, if anything, is hanging on from the past. If there is nothing hanging on and everything has been resolved, then we move on to whatever biblical knowledge is necessary to build character, create steps towards goals, and finally accomplish those goals. But if there is not resolution, then we must identify and move those stones, sometimes boulders, out of the way of forward movement.

How important is your past?

If you are an adult, your past was really important because you were, at one time, a child. But why is your childhood so important?

A study from the New York University Child Study Center states that

> "During the first five years, development proceeds at a pace faster than any other time of life. During this time children develop the social-emotional capacities that prepare them to be self-confident, trusting, empathic, intellectually inquisitive, competent and capable of understanding and adjusting well to others."[3]

A UNICEF report on Child Development and Early Learning states,

> "Recent research confirms that the first five years are particularly important for the development of the child's brain, and the first three years are the most critical in shaping the child's brain architecture. Early experiences provide the base for the brain's organizational development and functioning throughout life. They have a direct impact on how children develop learning skills as well as social and emotional abilities.[4]

Because generations typically carry the pain of a past generation forward, parents can easily be encumbered with their own pain—so much so that they fail to see the needs of their developing children. Also, there are circumstances that occur throughout life: traumatic events such as accidents, abuse, neglect, terror, and so on. These are events that mark our lives with beliefs at the moment of occurrence: things we believe about ourselves whether they are true or not. The enemy takes great advantage of these occasions, and if parents are not yielded to the Holy Spirit, they can completely miss the opportunities to tell children the truth about the circumstances and about themselves. When a parent does not step in with the truth, these deceptive beliefs will pile up in the memories of a child's life: beliefs they will have to confront at some point in the future.

After a traumatic event and after the enemy weaves a web of lies concerning the identity of his victims, he uses his influence to steer the victims into future circumstances that enforce the lies. The most recent circumstances add similar lies and drive the initial ones deeper into the victims' belief systems, compounding them. By the time people in these circumstances accept Christ, especially if they are older, they have a great deal of lies to confront in order to renew their minds.

Matthew 19:13-14 states,

> Then children were brought to him that he might lay his hands on them and pray. The disciples rebuked the people, but Jesus said, "Let the little children come to me and do not hinder them, for to such belongs the kingdom of heaven."

Some people, like me (as you will see in the next chapter), were targeted from birth. With others, however, their struggle began with a single event, and usually something very traumatic, occurring in childhood. I asked myself the question, "Why does the enemy target people in their childhood?" One reason, I believe, is because they have child-like faith. If children hear the truth at all in early childhood, they believe it lock, stock, and barrel. Children have great faith. It is for that reason that the enemy needs to confront those beliefs with an accident, a tragedy, a visitation, or even a serious misunderstanding. Through these events or circumstances, if no one comes behind them to bring clarity to the child's heart and mind, the enemy can sow seeds of doubt about the child's identity, worth, or ability to be loved. Typically, children between two and six years of age do not have the cognitive ability to determine who is at fault for any given situation. This is because they are in a stage of development where they are very self-conscious and generally unable to understand the point of view or perspective of others.[4] Small children attempt to make sense out of what is happening in their world by filling in the blanks with their own imagination, often with a strong sense of personal responsibility for what has taken place. The enemy is able to provoke "vain [useless, hopeless] imaginations" into the minds of mankind, especially children. Adults can and should actively take these imaginations captive through a dialogue with the child, since smaller children are usually not able to carry out this obedience for themselves (2 Corinthians 10:5).

The physical root of traumatic events

Command central for the human body is the brain. From the womb to the grave, the brain has an amazing ability to renew its structure and function and does so as a result of experience, especially emotional experience. This is the natural progression of the normal stress cycle, one that starts and stops.[5]

The traumatic neural breakdown caused by early life trauma mirrors that of traumatic breakdown caused by a chain of overwhelming events experienced later in life. The breakdown can be more severe when you begin life with a traumatic experience followed by a series of traumatic experiences. Stress symptoms range from those of PTSD, to depression, anxiety, learning problems, social disorders and chronic physical health problems.[6]

Trauma defined

Emotionally traumatizing events contain three common elements:
- The event is unexpected.

- The victim is unprepared.
- There is nothing the victim can do to prevent the event from occurring.

The impact of emotional and psychological trauma includes the following:
- Natural disasters, such as earthquakes, fires, floods, hurricanes, etc.
- Physical assault, including rape, incest, molestation, domestic abuse and serious bodily harm
- Serious accidents, such as automobile or other high-impact scenarios
- Experiencing or witnessing horrific injury, carnage or fatalities
- Falls or sports injuries
- Surgery, particularly emergency, and especially in first 3 years of life
- Serious illness, especially when accompanied by very high fever
- Birth trauma
- Hearing about violence to or sudden death of someone close

Research also shows that emotional trauma can result from such common occurrences such as:
- An auto accident
- The breakup of a significant relationship
- A humiliating or deeply disappointing experience
- The discovery of a life-threatening illness or disabling condition, or other similar situations

Source for developmental or relational trauma can result from:
- Forced separation very early in life from the primary caregiver
- Chronic mis-attunement of a caregiver to a child's attachment signals ("mal-attachment")

- Reasons such as neurological physical or mental illness, depression, grief or unresolved trauma
- Neurological disruption caused by experiences in the womb or during birth[7]

It was important for you to see these factors for a number of reasons. Firstly, they are going to show the glory of God in my testimony. Secondly, they demonstrate that it is by the grace of God and the power of intercession that many people are spared what could be a more devastating condition, both physically and mentally. Finally, they explain why there are so many more, (particularly in these final days prior to Christ's return–when deception is at an all-time high and the enemy knows that his time is short), who are struggling with mental illness, relational disorders, and demonic oppression.

What Should Be Our Response to Needing Help?

When we realize that we need help, the first thing we must do is admit our need. There are a great many reasons why people are afraid to admit their need for help. Some are afraid of what having a need means about them: being weak, being less than they feel that they should be, and the fear of vulnerability. Not confessing your need, however, can be very frustrating to your own life as well as those around you. You never hurt in a vacuum. Unless you are a hermit, the lack of response to your need for help is also hurting the ones you love. Besides your pain, you probably have a great many positive attributes, but they will pale in comparison to the weight of the problems for which you need help. Although some people may give you a wide berth of grace, many people will stumble over and react to your issues. Besides, there was a costly solution provided: the overcoming victory found in Christ.

I finally hurt badly enough as an adult that I had to admit my need. In the next several chapters that follow, I will use my life to illustrate how the enemy initiates his attack in childhood and continues it as far as he can through adulthood to destroy us if possible, to keep us from salvation, or at least to hinder us from our destiny in Christ. The enemy fears your purpose and your destiny. He understands that if you succeed, you are one more threat to his kingdom. His mission is to steal, kill, and destroy as much of your life as possible before he has to defend his kingdom's gates against the fruit of your destiny.

We are accountable for the truth that Christ won a great victory over sin and death through His death, burial, and resurrection. Therefore, we the church, must wake up to the reality of our need to ardently pursue whatever healing is necessary for our lives, lest we render the gospel impotent. He not only died to save us. He died to make us fruitful, abundant, and influential to this world with the love of God and the wisdom that comes from having the mind of Christ. In order to do this, we must carry Christ's delegated authority (Matthew 28:18-19) throughout the earth and declare the manifold wisdom of God to the rulers and authorities in the heavenly places. They need to know that we know who we are in Christ, and because Christ is unstoppable, so are we, in Him.

Are you saved, but ineffective in carrying out the great commission because of rejection, shame, fear, and the like? If so, please continue reading to see how the enemy fears your destiny and purposes to hold you back and render you as powerless as he can for as long as he can. This is why we need help. This is why we must admit our need.

Everybody has a story. Sometimes those stories are much more devastating than what you will read about in mine. The details are tragic, and I hear them all the time in my counseling practice. I weep with individuals as they relay their stories and witness the depths of pain they find the courage to admit. The answer for all of us who have a tragic story is the same: "For this purpose the Son of God manifested, that He might destroy the works of the devil" (1 John 3:8b).

Chapter One

Personal Application

1. What is another name for the Coach in John 14:26?

_____

2. Speaking from your own experience, would you agree that the enemy does not wait until we are grown to begin attacking our lives?   Yes   No

3. In Romans 8:38-39, what is the one thing Paul did not mention that cannot separate us from the love of God?

_____

4. How did Matthew Henry describe the way the Holy Spirit helps us renew our mind according to Romans 12:2?

_____

_____

5. Do you know, at this time in your life, that you are still battling the lies of the enemy?   Yes   No

6. Using the list provided in the section entitled, "Trauma defined" in this chapter, write down any traumatic experiences you suffered growing up.

_____

_____

7. What must we do when we realize that we need help?

_____

8. What solution was provided for any issues we may be carrying?

_____

Do We Need Help?

9. What is the enemy's mission?

_____

10. According to 1 John 3:8b, why did Jesus come to the earth?

_____

11. How would you describe our role in joining Christ in His work?

_____

_____

In Closing

Father, in the Name of Jesus, I pray for courage to flood the heart of the readers, as they continue reading this book. I ask that You, Holy Spirit, would keep their hearts open to the possibility of their need for Your help in identifying what could be holding them back from the Father's best plans for them. I pray that the final words of this chapter will incite them to go after their destiny as never before! Amen.

Chapter Two

THIS IS MY STORY

"Your eyes saw my unformed substance; in your book were written, every one of them, the days that were formed for me, when as yet there was none of them" (Psalm 139:16).

The Importance of Telling Your Story

Everyone has a story. Life stories are important. Besides being entertained, this may be why our culture loves television drama. You can learn a great deal about yourself by relating to another person's story. Likewise, you can learn a great deal about yourself by retelling your own story. For example, in working with my parents to correctly retell the events of my story, I learned some details that I did not know. Once I wrote them down, I retold them to my husband. When I did, I discovered that there were places in me that were still quite tender. By retelling the story, however, I was able to take a moment and allow the Coach to heal that place in my heart. It was a valuable experience!

In Philippians 3:13-14, the Apostle Paul states,

> Brothers, I do not consider that I have made it my own. But one thing I do: forgetting what lies behind

and straining forward to what lies ahead, I press on toward the goal for the prize of the upward call of God in Christ Jesus.

Some people have used this verse as a proof text to support the teaching that we should not look in the rear view mirror too intently. After all, are we not new creations in Christ? Is the old not gone? (2 Corinthians 5:17) In fact, as we are born again, we are new creations and the old man that was once dead in sin (Colossians 2:13) and cut off from the life of God the Father (Ephesians 4:18) is now a new creation because the presence of the Holy Spirit living inside of us (John 14:16-17). However, Paul was not referring to forgetting his painful past. In context, we read in this passage that he was perhaps referring to the joys of his flesh before Christ, but certainly his religious pedigree, and the accomplishments he had already achieved in Christ.[1] His point was not made in light of any pain he may have suffered growing up.

Some people are afraid of retelling their story because of how it defined them and how it still, perhaps, defines them today. Our story may describe us, but it does not have to define us unless we choose to allow it to do so.

Sometimes a person's story is so tragic and painful that he or she creates a new one. Then these people tell their imagined stories so many times and for so long, that the new story becomes their new reality. Why? It is because it gives them a new identity, one they are more comfortable embracing and sharing. It is amazing what the mind will do to escape the horror of emotional pain. Thank God that He made us with such ability. However, it is not meant to be the final solution. Remaining unresolved, the enemy can use the denial or the false identity to hold people captive to the lies that will never surface until they face the truth about their past and surrender it to Jesus for healing.

Some Christians may argue this point by saying that by Jesus' stripes, we have already been healed (Isaiah 53:5, 1 Peter 2:24). This is true. The day He was beaten and crucified, healing from the powerful grip of sin was made available for all mankind. However, it must be appropriated by each person who receives Christ. For it is all too easy to believe unto salvation, making Christ one's Savior, without entering into intimacy with Him: surrendering life's pain and the independent desires of the flesh unto His Lordship. To hold on to anything that He paid a precious price to redeem is to render His sacrifice less than what it was meant to accomplish.

God already knows everything about you, when you would come to know Him, and how to redeem your life from the destruction of sin in all the ways it has touched you. It is important not only to confess your sins unto salvation (1 John 1:9), but also to confess your weaknesses unto healing (James 5:16, Genesis 32).

We see this principle illustrated in the story of Jacob. Jacob spent years trying to hook and crook his way into an identity God had already declared over his life. He is like many of us today, feeling less than what the Father sees when He looks at us through the shed blood of His Son because we still see ourselves through the lens of our past, whether we are willing to admit it or not. This man, Jacob, gave us the first reference of the "house of God" where in a dream, he saw "the gate to heaven" with angels ascending and descending! He received this powerful vision and a promise from God about his destiny, and yet he still believed that he had to deceive his way to success (Genesis 28:10-22)!

Jacob finally became fed up with the mess he had made of his life. Between two wives, two concubines, twelve sons, overpopulated livestock, a father-in-law as deceptive as him, and the fear of his brother's revenge, he decided that he would find the Lord and demand his blessing! Even in the midst of all of his mess, we see that God's will was being accomplished, both in his life, and to fulfill the prophecy God had given to Abraham.

As Jacob traveled toward his destiny, He sent his wives, children, livestock, and all of his possessions ahead of him while he stayed back to seek God. Genesis 32:22-31 tells the story. The Pre-incarnate Jesus, described as a "man" in this passage (verse 24) and otherwise known throughout the Old Testament as "the LORD" or the "Angel of the Lord" (Genesis 16:7-14, Genesis 18, Judges 6:22; 13:21), meets Jacob and wrestles with Him throughout the night.[2]

Jacob demands his blessing before he will let go of the Lord, which is the same tenacity that we should employ in receiving our blessings! However, before the Lord will give Jacob his blessing, he asks Jacob an important question: "What is your name?" Did the Lord ask Jacob his name because he wanted to make his acquaintance? Indeed, the purpose of stating his name was so that Jacob could own and confess the sins of his reputation, signified by his name, which meant "supplanter/deceiver." Jacob was a con artist, but he grew tired of his own game.

Jacob had to confess this label and lay it down before God could change his name and before he could believe, receive, act upon, and enjoy the full expression of his new identity, which was Israel: "Who prevails with God" This is exactly why we must stay true to our own stories, and who we have become in the midst of them.

Allow the Lord to bring up gentle reminders of your own story as you are watching the enemy's plan unfold through my story.

A Safe Way to Tell Your Story

Step one: Start with counting your blessings and being grateful.

In spite of a long series of negative and sometimes traumatic experiences, I have many great childhood memories and a great deal for which to be thankful. I am an only child who grew up in a large extended family of faithful church-attenders. I received a strong foundation of faith and good will toward others. There was a general sense of love, although it was not always spoken or demonstrated. I only remember one time that I doubted being loved by my parents. On that one occasion, my mother reassured me, and it worked. All of my physical needs were met. We went on family vacations most of my years at home. I had best friends and neighbors with swimming pools. I was taught to work hard. I was not given everything without the opportunity to earn an allowance through responsibilities at home or in my mother's or father's business. Faithfulness in lay ministry was modeled before me in so many ways that I have loved the ministry my entire life. Fellowship and fun with other believers was a big part of my early development. My grandparents and my parents took in wayward children, struggling single parents and their children, missionaries, drunks or drug addicts, foster children, and dying relatives. To this day, my heart has so much room to take people in, and I have done it for years. For all the ways the enemy was able to attack me throughout my life, I am grateful for the good things I "caught" observing and serving with my family.

Step two: Understand why the good memories are harder to recall than the bad ones.

As the enemy's assaults piled up through the years, I easily lost sight of the good memories and focused mostly on the bad memories. No one that I have ever met is devoid of any bad memories, even if these were only a matter of an accident or a misunderstanding. For some, life can be so bad for so long that all they have to focus on is bad memories. For others, life could have been mostly good, and so those people might write off their bad experiences as typical. However, in either case, it is not the events that matter so much, but rather the reaction to each event and beliefs that are formed in the process. Wrong beliefs can shape your thinking for years. These patterns of thinking are why our minds must be renewed once we come to Christ. Renewing my mind was my deepest need, and thankfully my Coach came to my rescue and helped me in a way that was powerfully effective over time and most meaningful to me.

Step three: Understand who is really at fault for your bad memories.

If I had written this story several years ago, I am sure I would have told it differently. Thank God for a cleansed perspective as I share this with you today! Now more than ever, I realize who was really to blame for my misfortune. I have more understanding today than ever that, "...we do not wrestle against flesh and blood, but against the rulers, authorities, cosmic powers over this present darkness, against the spiritual forces of evil in heavenly places" (Ephesians 6:12). As a young woman with a great deal of experience with darkness and little knowledge about how the enemy works through people, I easily blamed people for my pain, instead of the enemy. However, thanks to my Coach, I saw the truth in Luke 23:34 when Jesus uttered the following words as He hung on the cross staring at the crowd, who had agreed, even conspired, to hang Him there. He said, "Father, forgive them [the Jews, the Romans, the people; emphasis mine], for they do not know what they are doing."

Jesus knew that the human, heathen rulers of this world would have never killed Him had they really believed that He was the King of glory. More importantly, however, the mystery of the wisdom of Christ's coming was hidden throughout the ages past from not only the human, heathen rulers, but also the spiritual rulers of this world. If either of them had known who He was, "they would not have crucified the Lord of glory" (1 Corinthians 2:6-8), as it was through the sinless life and ultimate sacrificial death of Christ, that he would destroy the works of the enemy. So the next time you are being attacked by someone, whether verbally or worse, think about who is really in control.

Step four: Seek to know what is so important that the enemy may have attacked your life so severely (other than the fact that he hates you, of course).

There was a great deal of spiritual warfare surrounding my life from the time I was born. Today, I believe I have a bit of insight as to why that happened. Several years ago, I was seeking the Lord in regard to how I would specifically walk in my destiny. From my early teens, I instinctively knew the answers to people's problems. Once I was baptized in the

Holy Spirit, I noticed an increase in this gift. Then, when I began to seek confirmation about my destiny, I felt strongly led in the direction of discipleship counseling. It was at this time, as I prayed, two things emerged of which I was not previously aware. They were actually great confirmations! First, my dad told me that before I was born, he instinctively knew that I would be a girl and that my name was to be Monica Ann. Second, my husband bought me one of those little cards with the meaning of your name on it. In Greek, the name Monica means "alone, advisor," both of which describe my life in great detail. In Latin it means, "To advise, counselor." In Spanish, it means "counselor." After all I had been through, I was overjoyed to finally have some clarity!

Setting the Stage

The spiritual root: Lies! Lies! Lies!

It always amazes me how people, who appeared to have a good life growing up, experienced various types of trauma when you look beneath the surface to discover what is troubling them in the present. This was certainly true in my case. Amidst all of the great things that I observed and learned growing up, I am going to illustrate how the enemy targeted my life and assaulted me in such a succession of attacks, it is almost unbelievable looking back. I truly believe that, through the lies that he worked to imbed into my mind, his intention was that I would be paralyzed by fear and feeling mentally incompetent and emotionally crippled as a result of his onslaught. But thankfully, I have the mind of Christ (1 Corinthians 2:16) and last time I checked, He is not crazy! That truth is one of our Kingdom benefits. I held on to the Word, declaring that I have the mind of Christ and allowed the Coach to give me an experience of truth in places of the painful events that occurred throughout my life. This is how I overcame and how I have seen many people overcome the mental instability that occurs due to years of what I am about to unfold in the next few sections of this chapter.

If we trust the Coach's help to overcome the struggles we have faced throughout our lives, God will give us authority in those areas in which we struggled. Since I came to understand this scheme of the enemy, I have often seen it in the history of many clients. Without the use of suggestion and after hearing their story, I point this out so that they can see how this series of events and circumstances has reinforced the same lies over and over again. This is why, for them, biblical truth seems more challenging to embrace than it should be.

Emotionally out of bounds

Fear became deeply rooted in my mind, but it went far beyond rational fear. I meet so many people who are dealing with fear and in fact, Luke 21:25-26 warns that fear will increase as we move closer to the coming of the Lord.

> And there will be signs in sun and moon and stars, and on the earth distress of nations in perplexity because of the roaring of the sea and the waves, people fainting with fear and with foreboding of what is coming on the world. For the powers of the heavens will be shaken.

I want to give you an illustration of this principle of fear and other emotions outside of their rational boundaries. Fear is part of our nature. It is part of our emotional make-up. It is also a component of the first level of stress to which God designed our bodies to respond. When someone is in danger or afraid, the brain, particularly the hypothalamus, sends the response message to two body systems to release the appropriate hormones to initiate the "fight or flight" response. Heart rate and blood pressure rise to get the body moving if necessary. Once the danger is over, the body goes back to normal. The stress cycle is like a loop that starts and stops as necessary.

Fear, anger, grief, and envy are all "normal" brain/body responses to life. I like to illustrate these emotions as characters playing in the safety of a fenced-in back yard. As long as they stay in the backyard, meaning that they have a rational beginning and an end, they are fine. We become afraid, and then our fear is alleviated. We become angry, but we resolve our anger. We lose someone and we grieve and the grief comes to an end. That is rational. However, when those characters get out of control and go beyond the boundary of the fenced yard, they are open game to spiritual forces that prey upon them. The enemy takes our thoughts to a whole new level, suggesting things that are irrational. In other words, fear can become energized by a spirit of fear (2 Timothy 1:7). Now the cycle does not necessarily start and stop. It starts and keeps on going, making us a fearful person rather than occasionally experiencing fear. This is where I have ministered to a great number of people over the last fifteen years, and it is also where I was by the time I was eight years old. I had become like a wounded animal: the vultures were already picking at my mind, and more were circling. However, the imbedded memories that were yet to be burned into my mind would eventually become the raw material through which God would fashion my weaponry for the future.

Something that may be of value to know is that when we venture outside this fenced boundary in our emotions, if we are doing it in pride, the enemy can become involved with our behavior in such a way that causes us to stumble into sins that we no longer see as sinful. For example, let's look at someone in a position of authority like a security guard. If the guard does not immediately deal with issues such as anger and control as soon as they occur, and if the guard continues to ignore his need for resolution, he could easily move outside of the protected area into the extreme. As he moves past the protected boundary, the enemy can easily energize the guard's emotions, taking them to limits that an observer might see, but the guard may not easily recognize as he loses control and offends or even injures someone. Someone in close relationship to the guard may be able to bring the heightened emotions to his attention successfully. If not, then the one in close relationship to the guard could pray and intercede for him. Now the officer may, perhaps, feel the Holy Spirit's conviction, or the Lord may respond by arranging a simple wake-up call that gets the guard's attention. At this level, the guard can respond through simple repentance. However, I have seen and experienced this type of stronghold taken to levels that have required agreement and specific ministry to bring the individual back into a place of peace and more balanced behavior.

As I retell my story, you will see how most of the traumatic events defined in chapter one were part of my experience and how the enemy meant to use them to my detriment. However, I hope you will also notice how the Holy Spirit manifested His presence and His power in the background of my experience. Throughout all of your life, particularly if you have received Christ, will receive Christ, or if someone is interceding for you; no matter what happens, the Coach, as well as angelic activity, are at work on your behalf.

This is My Story

Born through adversity

My mother struggled with poor health throughout her childhood and into early adulthood. She was a twin and the only one to survive a rare stomach disorder. Her sister died by the time she was eight months of age. Mom had a calcium deficiency and lost all of her teeth by the time she was fourteen. She had a difficult time finishing her education due to missing so many days of school. Two days after my parents wed, she suffered a mild heart attack and was hospitalized.

By the time she became pregnant with me, she was working as a civil servant for the Air Force where my dad was stationed in Newport News, Virginia. She is a very petite woman and I was a very large baby as I take after my dad's side of the family. He jokingly says that when he was born, he weighed twelve pounds, had two teeth, and hair on his legs!

Mom had a severe iron deficiency and battled fatigue. At the end of her pregnancy, she was forced to change physicians and became the patient of an extremely non-compassionate doctor. Her water broke three weeks before I was born. Water breaking before thirty-seven weeks increases the risk of improper lung development, increased bacterial infection, and greater pressure on the head during delivery.[3] Giving birth was extremely hard on her and very stressful for me.

Infant abuse

As mom's maternity leave was nearing an end, she had to find a childcare provider for me so that she could go back to work. She found a young military wife with no children who was willing to watch me during work hours. When I was about three months old, my mom discovered severe bruises on my body and realized that the sitter was abusing me. Lacking confidence in finding a safe environment for me, my parents decided that the best solution would be to send me to live with trusted family members who were the closest to the base, which was about two hours away.

Early abandonment

At three months of age, I was taken a couple hours away to live with my grandparents. I would see my parents only on the weekends until my dad was discharged and they moved back home. I am certain I missed my parents, but my grandparents loved me and treated me as their own. My uncle was only five when I was born, so he became like a big brother in the early years. My granny became like a second mom.

Quiet, contented, and sickly

Once my dad was discharged from the military, together, my parents and grandparents settled on a large piece of property which became affectionately known as Dennis Hollow. The county finally named the road into our property "Irvenway Lane" after my grandfather. It was a great place for kids with plenty of land, a large garden, fields, and wooded areas.

Soon my parents found jobs at a local chemical plant. As usual, my days were spent on our little family farm, in the care of my granny. Our house sat right beside my grandparents' house.

I was quiet and easy going. While my uncle was in school, I spent hours outside with my grandmother in the large garden. I would sit on a five-gallon bucket while she worked each row, perfectly content, she said. I would also run through the laundry while she hung it on the line. Inside, I watched her cook three meals each day, helped her with my little iron and board, or played in her button collection while she sewed. I also followed my grandfather around the farm feeding the chickens, watching him with the rabbits, or feeding and butchering the hogs. Otherwise, I roamed the land, catching bees in a jar and pretending it was my radio, playing in the old buildings and scattered old trucks, or atop of the chicken house, which was my "fort."

Conversations were practically non-existent. If you said much at all, adults just patted your head and smiled at you or talked to each other over you. That was my only pet peeve. Once Granny became the official Nanny to more grandchildren, my grandfather did not like for us to talk much indoors. "Hush up that fuss!" was his favorite phrase. Even when he got cancer and they had to remove his vocal chords, he still used one of our toys called the "Mystic Writing Pad" where you drew on a thin sheet of plastic with a little stylus. He would write "Hush!" in bold letters and rip the sheet up to make a loud noise for emphasis. We did, however, have a very large basement to run and play in when it rained, and we spent hours outside from sun up to sun down when it was clear. We knelt to pray before meals in their home and we were never allowed to speak much at the table, although we always tried to make each other laugh so as to get someone in trouble.

I got very sick once a year in the winter, experiencing febrile convulsions with repeated bouts of pneumonia. Mom and Dad had to put me in ice to try and bring my fever down. This was frightening to them and alienating for me as I made annual hospital trips for oxygen tent therapy from age two to five.

I still remember sitting in my hospital bed, a large square tent zipped around the entire bed like *The Boy in the Plastic Bubble.* Mom and Dad took turns sitting with me day and night every year. I was made an honorary doctor and given a small plastic medical bag with a toy stethoscope, reflex tester, shots, and Band-Aids.

Fears and phobias

When I was four years old, two significant things happened. First, I was dancing a little jig on the ledge of our basement stairwell. I was boasting the fact that I got to stay home while my uncle and my cousin had to go to school. As they walked out of ear-shot, I slipped and fell into the stairwell catching myself by the fingertips. There I hung, calling out for help for what seemed like an eternity. Granny must have heard me calling out as she went to hang clothes on the line. She walked down the stairs until she could reach me and carry me to safety. She sat me down on the carport and said something like, "Goodness gracious, are you okay?" I breathlessly sobbed and said, "Yes ma'am." She said, "Good." Then she turned me around and thankfully wore me out. I never danced on that ledge again.

Then, on a day when my Daddy was home from work with the flu, I went across the field to feed the dog. Our dog, Bobo, was fenced in a pen built onto the side of one of the old buildings. He was barking more than normal, but I thought he was glad to see me, so I stood on a cinderblock to reach over the fence to pet him. It was then that I heard a rattling noise. I looked and there was a rattlesnake poised and ready to strike only inches from my leg. I did what any four-year old would do. I screamed and ran. However, in my mind I thought if I ran past him and around the truck, it would confuse him and he would not chase after me. So I did. There was either an angel blocking the strike or he was one slow snake! I ran to the house screaming and crying for my Dad to go and rescue Bobo. He quickly put on his clothes and shoes and grabbed a hoe as we ran across the field. Finding the snake still in position because of the barking dog, Daddy swung the hoe and cut off his head and threw him up in a tree. Looking back, it was like the enemy, hiding under the familiar cloak of the serpent. His plan was foiled that day, but he began to plot his revenge.

Once I began school, I got sick for a variety of reasons, one of which was fear. In Kindergarten, I became too afraid to go on a school trip. The teacher had to take me off the bus and call my grandfather to come and get me. That memory is so vivid that I remember what I was wearing and how my hair was fixed, and I remember the fear like it was yesterday. I was gripped by a sudden, strong sense of insecurity.

Westward Ho!

At age seven, my family relocated away from our friends and family. My dad was invited to leave his job at the local plant and move us to Ridgecrest, California to work with a friend who was a pastor and the foreman for local construction. Moving meant we had to move from the East Coast, where our entire family lived, to the Mohave Desert on the West Coast. It was extremely underdeveloped, and Dad was going to help build. It was like moving to the moon – literally. The show *Lost in Space* was being filmed just miles from the ranch that we eventually rented. The interestingly shaped rocks in the show were not props; they were unusual desert rocks in a place called "The Pinnacle."

Earthquake!

When we first arrived, my parents stayed in the RV we drove from Virginia to California. They were welcomed to park it at the pastor's home. I stayed inside the house and slept on the couch one night. Initiation to our lunar village came early one morning shortly after 6:00 a.m. when the couch I was sleeping on began to move across the floor. I escaped the furniture carousel in the living room and ran outside where I witnessed the rocks dancing in the driveway. Then I ran around the corner of the house and my parent's RV was swaying back and forth, but there was no wind blowing. I immediately thought it was the Rapture of the Church, which was often preached and the subject of gospel music at that time. This was it for me, so I began to jump up and down, fearful that I was not ready. Finally, others began to emerge from the house. We were just hours away from the BIG earthquake that wrecked Los Angeles in 1971. By the next day, I am sure adults were watching the reports of the devastation on television. However, life went on for me as if nothing happened at all. No one offered any explanation and I did not ask, but it added greatly to my fear and insecurity.

Space camp

Mom enrolled me in school. I left the "normal" school with all of my friends in Virginia to attend a school that was more like a hotel, in that you entered each classroom from the outside. The other kids did not talk to me much, as I came in the middle of the year and they were quite territorial. I will never forget standing on the playground and hearing a siren go off. Everyone started screaming and running for the classroom. I stood there dumbfounded until a teacher grabbed me. As we stood by the classroom window, we watched the sand storm come and go. I was afraid. By the time the storm finished, recess was also over and we walked outside to the library/cafeteria to get graham crackers and milk. After snack, we went home. I do not remember doing any work at that school. I do not remember one conversation with a teacher or students. My only memories were reading in the library, recess, sand storms, eating snack, and taking home a permission slip one day.

The permission slip was to get on a bus to another nearby school and get a vaccination. I just knew that my mother would never agree to anything so horrible! Back home, I had to sit on the teacher's lap when it came time to get shots at school. I cried and cried. My mom knew this! When she signed the permission slip, I just stood in shock. She was actually going to send me to who-knows-where with who-knows-who and be exposed to who-knows-what! She matter-of-factly said, "Take this back to school tomorrow. Give it to your teacher." I said nothing, but knew I had to have a plan. The next day we got on a bus. Remembering it now feels like a scene from the Disney movie, *"Holes."* I could envision us being taken to Camp Greenlake where we might never return. We arrived at a high school where we were assembled in a gymnasium with a lot of other children both young and old. To my horror, they were using guns and shooting everyone in the arm. Everybody screamed or hollered when they were "shot." I ducked under a skirted table and hid until I could creep back into the line getting back on the bus. I did not tell my mother for years!

Sand storms, horned toads, and weird kids

We lived a long way out of the smallest town I had ever seen. Sometimes it was challenging to get to town because you might be stopped on the highway for over half an hour waiting on a giant tortoise to cross! So, we sometimes visited our closest neighbor. She was a painter and lived in a beautiful Spanish home with a center courtyard. She was married and her husband had no voice box but spoke through a gadget he held up to his trachea hole. He sounded like a robot to me. Her son was a child prodigy and just a few years older than I. He spent his time in a science lab adjacent to his bedroom. The woman was nice. Everyone else was very strange to me. The boy accompanied me in the desert together on a few occasions, teaching me about the reptiles and animals. However, I saw him so little that I do not even recall his name.

I watched a lot of television in California. Besides playing at the stables, the outdoors was full of sand storms, snakes, horned toads, wild dogs, and weird kids. For fun, my parents took me to a Tuesday evening rodeo where people sat their toddlers on the corral fence with beer in their bottles. I liked animals and I liked the rodeo, so I became a cattle girl. I had the job of stinging steers in the rump when they did not want to travel up the chute to be released and roped. I sometimes even worked inside the ring with the live action! Animals had a way of making me feel better and they were usually quite responsive to me.

If most things were not already terrifying and weird enough by this time, we went on vacation to a rodeo where *The Great Suicide Race,* starring Cliff Robertson, was filmed. We stayed in our RV and I got to wear jeans and a matching shirt with cowboy boots and a cowboy hat. This started a new trend since we were Pentecostal and, back in Virginia, I did not normally wear much other than skirts and dresses. During the rodeo, "Grandmother Goose", a white Brahma Bull, threw her rider and chased him to the fence and drove her horn through his arm. This shed a whole new light on my job as a rodeo girl. I thought getting hit with a few volts of electricity when I jumped onto the fence to get away from one of the steers was bad! Seeing that guy pinned through the arm to the fence made quite the impression, and I do not remember participating in the rodeo after that trip.

Stalked by nature

When we arrived home, we were soon to discover that when you leave your house vacant for any length of time, the critters move in. I was sitting across a winged back chair one Saturday after we returned. My dad was going to sneak up behind me and scare me. Instead, he grabbed me by the arm and slung me across the room! I screamed and began to cry because it shocked me and it hurt. It was then that I saw him pointing to the ugliest creature I had ever seen. On the top of the chair above where I was sitting, there was a Vinegaroone. It is a large spider that looks like a Scorpion, also known as a whip scorpion. It has a long, whip-like tail that emits a burning, vinegar smelling fluid to ward off its prey. It is non-poisonous, but it has pinchers and if you get sprayed, it stings. This gave me the creeps! That night, when I pulled the covers down to get into bed, I am glad I looked before I leaped because there was a Vinegaroone under my covers. Was it just me or were these creatures only in my personal space? They were nowhere else to be found in our home.

One day soon after the Vinegaroone incident, Mom sent me home from the stables. Our house was not more than 200 yards and perpendicular to the stables and, as I was walking home, out of nowhere came this wild dog. I have never been afraid of dogs in my life, but this dog was no ordinary dog. He looked more like a Hyena, and he was none too happy. As I came around one side of the stables, he was running from the direction of the other side, so I started running. Of course, my decision to run may have made the situation worse, but what other decision is a seven year old going to make? He chased me all the way to the house and up onto the patio. I grabbed the doorknob just as he lunged and put a claw in the back of my knee before I went through the door and slammed it shut. I have no idea where the dog went. I was bleeding, but afraid to go and get my parents. Soon after, they arrived home. They did not see the dog, but Mom bandaged my leg to get the bleeding to stop. My insecurities were growing and these events occurred within a few weeks before what would become the main event for my life in California.

Struck down but not destroyed!

We had a few horses in Virginia so I was accustomed to riding with my dad. In California, I also rode with my dad. One day, just after my eighth birthday, Dad decided it was time for me to learn to ride on my own. He secured a trainer to give me lessons and I was riding alongside him. There were several who went on this particular ride, but Mom remained at the stable. I rode Rowdy, a beautiful reddish-brown quarter horse. He was an older horse and not terribly huge, but I was only eight, so he was a giant to me. We set out as a group and had not gone too many miles from the stable. The group trotted a bit faster, and my trainer was also riding just ahead of me. My horse continued to walk and fall behind, and that was fine with me – the slower the better! Suddenly, Rowdy whinnied loud, and I spotted a rattlesnake at this feet. He reared up, and I got scared because I seemed very high off the ground (heights – snakes – Deja-vu). Rowdy wheeled around and began to run like lightening. I recall that it looked to me like the old western movies: the cowboy is riding fast, and you see the scenery flying by. It was blinding, and I had no idea what direction we were headed. My feet had come out of the stirrups and were flailing. The trainer chased us on a racing horse and still could not catch up! He called out to me, "Hold on! Hold on!" I held on to horn, hair, reigns, and anything I could. I pressed my legs as tightly as I could to his sides and I slid sideways until I finally slid underneath his running feet. By no fault of his own, he trampled my head.

There I was, lying in the desert sand with my head laid open by a perfect horse hoof-shaped cut. The right side of my skull was depressed against my brain. Part of it was crushed. I was unconscious. Meanwhile, Rowdy went straight back to the stables, walked over and stood by my mom. Seeing that I was not with him, she jumped into our gold Cadillac and tore out into the desert to find me. When she arrived, a man who lived nearby had already reached me and would not let mom touch or move me. She said that she had never felt so helpless in her life.

This Is My Story

Miracles in the desert

I was picked up by ambulance that afternoon and taken to the tiny hospital in Ridgecrest. They had no means to do much for me other than to place me in ICU with an I.V. that would keep my brain from swelling and causing brain damage. They would transport me to Bakersfield, which was a three hour drive, only if I came out of a coma. The situation was grave.

So there I lay. Dad said that my head was swollen and my face was black and blue. My long brown hair was matted with dirt and blood. Everyone thought I would die, so mom called everyone she knew in town and all of our family on the East Coast to pray. I had prayer going up from New York to Virginia, and all the way down to Florida.

By the next morning, at exactly 3:50 a.m., my dad witnessed a miracle. Like time-lapsed photography, as Dad described it, the bruising completely left my face and I woke up and told them all about That was miracle number one.

The next thing I remember, I was in the ambulance on my way to Bakersfield. I awakened and tried to lift my head. It hurt really badly. I called out to the nurse thinking she was my mom, but quickly slipped back out of consciousness. I would not wake up again for days after surgery.

Once in Bakersfield, tests began to assess the damage. Part of the cerebral cortex, in the area of the injury, was mangled and cut by the horse's hoof. Also, part of the skull had been crushed and would need to be removed. The surgeon said to my parents, "I do not know what kind of people you are, but if you believe in prayer, you might want to start now. If she lives, she could be a vegetable the rest of her life. The best case scenario will be that she will suffer with seizures the rest of her life." Dad responded by assuring the surgeon that he was a witness when God healed me earlier that morning. After surgery, the doctor reported to my parents that God indeed had His hand on me. Once inside my skull, even though they had to do what was considered five major surgeries through one incision, the doctor found greater ease and results than he expected. The cerebral cortex was repaired and able to come together nicely without damaging my eyesight. He cleaned the area of the brain that had been cut and quickly removed the fractured skull, which left a nice-sized hole for any brain swelling that would occur. I would go without that part of my skull for a year, followed by an additional surgery one year later to insert a plate that would be placed over the hole and wired to the surrounding skull.

Someone watching over me

I remember that while I was under heavy medication from the surgery, I could hear people talking. I asked my mom just recently if she read to me before I awakened. She said, "As a matter of fact I did! I read Bible stories to you." I remember hearing other people: nurses, and doctors. But I also remember Jesus being in the room. I could not see Him, but I could sense His presence. I was in pain, and I often received shots. I had paper stars all over my wall for each shot I received and did not cry. Mostly, it was because I was not awake.

After I woke up, I was still in a lot of pain. One day, the nurse came to give me a shot. I could still feel Jesus in the room. I said, "Can you please lay your hand on me and ask Jesus to heal me?" The nurse gave me the pain shot and left the room. Later, she found my Mom and cried, confessing that she was a Christian but had so little faith that she was afraid to pray for me. She apologized. Mom and Dad said that several miracles surrounding my injury happened while I was in the hospital.

God definitely had his hand on our family. Dad's work situation was changing just before I was hurt. He did not know what he was going to do. A man who was admitted to ICU alongside me was so touched by my situation that he sent for my dad to visit him after he was placed on another floor. He told dad that he was so moved by what happened to me and how I conducted myself after I came out of the coma that he wanted to offer Dad a job for as long as he might remain in Ridgecrest.

However, while I was in the hospital, my mom's dad suffered a massive heart attack while on vacation in Florida. Due to the condition of my grandfather, along with our need for family support, the chances of our remaining in California for much longer were slim. It would greatly depend on my recovery.

Miraculously, just two weeks after surgery, I was released from the hospital, but as much as my mother would have liked to go home, the doctor would not allow me to travel for at least three months to watch my progress. We traveled less and lived a much quieter life. Mom was a civil servant at the China Lake Naval Weapons Air Station before the accident and her employer thankfully held her job while she had to be away during my hospital stay. She was able to return to work and found a precious pastor's wife to watch me on base while she worked.

It's the little things in life

My sitter was a "little person" married to a very tall man. She looked strange to me, was my height, and very playful. I had never seen a little person before, but staying with her turned out to be one of the bright spots during my time in California.

This sweet lady played games with me most of the day: jacks, hide and seek, and ball games. Whenever she had to attend to her adult responsibilities, she handed me large box of colorful IBM punch cards. She would always make sure the colors were mixed up so that I could dump them out on the carport and spend a lot of time putting them back in order. I loved those cards and I loved that woman.

Eastward Ho!

It seemed our frightening experiences were not over. One Saturday, shortly before we moved, my dad was on the patio using a skill saw. Suddenly, we heard him screaming, "Help! Help! Help! Help!" We ran out onto the patio and he was being electrocuted. Mom ran over and kicked the plug out of the socket and it stopped. We were all breathless. Dad was nervously laughing, Mom was hyperventilating and I was ready to leave California!

I was not allowed to fly, so air travel was out of the question. My dad purchased a Cadillac and I rode all the way to the east coast lying in the back seat. Dad struggled to follow behind us in the truck because my mom's lead foot revealed her anxiety about getting home.

Is that the same girl?

One of the most painful moments after waking up after surgery was to discover my hair hanging in a bag on the foot of the hospital bedrail. My head was shaved! I looked like a boy! What would life be like for me now?

Once back in Virginia, we moved back to the same little county. Although we bought a house in a different neighborhood, instead of moving back to Dennis Hollow, I was zoned for the same school. We also returned to our old church. The only difference was that now, I was bald and looked like a cancer patient. I would have to wear a helmet for a year while my brain swelling went down. I would have a body guard at school that next Fall to protect me.

I did not have a body guard on the bus, so I had to sit just behind the driver. One day a boy on my bus, one who knew me before I moved to California, thought I was faking (as if a girl would wear a helmet every day for no good reason). He removed my helmet and hit me on the head really hard. Either God protected me or he threw a lousy punch because it hurt my feelings more than my head, and I still had no skull on the injured side where he struck me. I will never forget, my bus driver slammed on the brakes and put that boy off on the highway, making him walk the rest of the way home. Seeing that I was fine other than crying from embarrassment and rejection, she put my helmet back on and finished the bus route. Life was different back then. I guess she figured if the boy told on her for putting him off the bus, he knew he would also have to own the cruel, dangerous thing he had done to me as well. I did not tell my mom. I was afraid we would all somehow get in trouble. My bus driver still had her job the next day and the boy was back on the bus again too. It was like nothing had ever happened. In fact, he ignored me the rest of our school years together. He represented a host of kids who either made fun of me or ignored me. Bullies are not nice and many kids and adults alike act out around things that do not make sense or are hard to explain. I was the same girl they knew, but I was so different from what they remembered. Because I was quiet, I was an easy target.

Double exposure

Shortly after we returned from California, our family reconnected with a young family we had known prior to our departure. It was not uncommon for my parents to allow me to visit with them or run errands with the wife.

One day, on such an occasion with this woman, while we were driving, she pulled a magazine out from under her seat and laid it in my lap. As I flipped through it, I began to feel very strange. It was a Playgirl magazine and I did not notice at first, but the man on the cover had on an open trench coat and was otherwise nude. I closed the magazine and laid it face down on the seat beside me. She made a smirking comment that I do not remember. I nervously laughed it off and said nothing more about it. I never asked to go anywhere else with her or to stay with them again.

My parents had no idea this happened because I was too ashamed to tell them. I was never drawn to look at pornography ever again, even to this day. However, this is not the case for so many others.

In his book, *Treating Pornography Addiction: The Essential Tools for Recovery*, Dr. Kevin B. Skinner states,

"In a majority of cases, the earlier the exposure to pornography, the deeper the client's level of addiction. In most cases I see involvement with pornography starting between ages ten to fourteen. Children get exposed to pornography at a friend's house, an older brother's magazine stash, a parent's TV, R-rated movies, the Sears catalog, advertisements, and most recently, online via pornographic emails, pop-up windows, and in some cases by accident.

In today's society each of us is constantly being exposed to some form of sexual image or sexual innuendo. Our children are no different. They are being forced to deal with sexual issues long before they should be. An eight year old should not be exposed to a parent's X-rated videos. Children should not be exposed to unwanted sexual images over the Internet, but they are. One researcher found that one in four children who use the internet is exposed to unwanted sexual material (as cited in Buford, *Your Children & Pornography: A Guide for Parents*, 2001)."[4]

Am I sick?

With the type of injury I sustained, there was a 99.9% chance of suffering with epilepsy for the rest of my life. Therefore, over the next five years, I had to go back to the hospital twice a year and undergo tests to determine if I was experiencing irregular brain rhythms. I had to have an EEG, and it always seemed to be storming when I went. They wanted me to go to sleep while I was being tested, but it was always difficult because I was afraid. I had to strip down to my underwear and walk a taped line to check my balance. I had to touch the doctor's finger and touch my nose and other such repetitive tests. God had healed me, and my case defied the normal prognosis. If I had been who I am now, it would have boosted my faith, and I would have used it for a witness every time I went back to that hospital. However, being who I was then, I was as afraid as everyone else that something might still happen to me if I pushed the boundaries. Even though the tests were always inconclusive to show that there was any problem, no one pushed me to test my limits and I was afraid to push myself. It would take me years to discover that I actually had more physical capacity than before the accident and that I was much more intelligent than I or my teachers believed I was in secondary school.

Expanding the family

The following year, my parents filed papers trying to adopt a child, but the state suggested that they become foster parents instead. Our first case would be two sisters who the state did not want to separate. The girls had been living in torment with a single mom who had serious issues and various men in and out of the home. We lived in a tri-level home at the time. When the girls moved in, my parents moved downstairs and the girls and I lived upstairs. I had fun with them. They were good company for me. But too often, their problems flared up. The younger had more obvious problems. She was cross-eyed, and not a day went by when she had not destroyed something at school or was in trouble for one reason or another. She threw up a lot and did not speak very well. When her mother would come for a supervised visit, she would hold on to the door handle of the car as her mom drove away until she had to let go. It broke my heart and made me cry. Mom and Dad were so kind to her. They paid for the surgery to repair her eyesight.

It was a blessing for these girls to live with us. They had deep needs, and my parents loved them as their own. Their lives manifested the emotional, mental, physical, and sexual fallout of the abuse and supernatural encounters experienced in their home of origin. Sharing a floor of our home with them, I did not weather their storms unscathed.

The older girl was almost a teenager. One evening, we girls were home alone. Whether she was faking or serious, I do not know, but I was terrified as she started having a flashback or she was hallucinating. I don't remember if we watched something on television that triggered her or what caused it, but she was out of control, and the younger girl and I were afraid. She was screaming and pointing as if she saw something or someone. She ran downstairs to the kitchen and got a butcher knife out of the drawer and threw it at the apparition she saw. I told Dad, more for her sake than mine, but I am sure there was little that could be done other than to make sure she was alright. Some things happened in our home that my parents did not know about until recently. I never told some of them. I was afraid to tell.

The girls went with us to church, but there were state regulations that limited what foster parents could do in regard to spiritual matters, even if they had known what to do for them. Sometimes when you are trying to do something good, like fostering children, you invite certain resistance and retaliation from the enemy to work through the misfortune and emotional trauma of the children you are trying to help. It is something for which fostering families, as well as adopting families, need to be prepared, especially if you already have children in the home.

A year and a half later, the girls returned to their mother. They called about two months later. They were afraid and saying, "Dad, can you come and get us? But the state had closed our case with them and had strictly forbidden my parents to have any more contact with them.

A short time later, my parents accepted another foster assignment. She was a senior in High School and would only stay until her graduation. I really admired her, as she was beautiful and respectful to my parents. One evening close to when she would leave, we were home alone. She innocently introduced me to the Ouija Board game. I am sure she thought it was all in fun, but for me, all hell broke loose after that.

Darkness closes in

At the time, I was born again. I did not have a rebellious nature—always a good kid. I did not intentionally go after darkness, but it came after me. After that, I began to have dreams, visions, and visitations. There were many nights I woke my mom to pray with me so that I could sleep peacefully. I had one recurring dream night after night where death would visit and say, "I can have you any time I want." I would wake up and see shadows about the room. I did not sleep well.

Dad's business kept him away quite a bit. This increased as the years went by. Speaking from a counselor's viewpoint, I know that the historical issues, extended family issues, and the stress surrounding my life must have taken a toll on my parent's marriage. Mom was still in the ministry and it was a challenging season in that arena as well. Our family tradition was more about toughing things out. Commitment was a core value of their generation. As a result, there was an unspoken tension in our home. Whether you are open about your stress and conflict with your children, many of them are very sensitive to the lack of peace at home. They may not be able to articulate the problem exactly, but they can sense when something is off balance and it can affect their sense of security.

Too close for comfort

When I was ten, a young man from our community came to our church looking for the preacher's daughter. She and her family were our neighbors. She had evidently befriended this troubled young man. I imagine she had reached out to him and perhaps had invited him to church. My mom was the Daycare Director at the time, and it was common for me to ride the bus route with her and help out at work. This particular day, I was alone downstairs in the church basement, cleaning a playroom while the children were upstairs at lunch. It was a partial cinderblock room with one door. This young man came downstairs and opened the door, walked just inside the door and shut and locked it behind him. I stood frozen across the room and began to feel creepy and afraid. I watched his face change from his normal, weird look to a more serious, sinister look. It was as if his eyes changed. He reached down and picked up a wooden rocking chair and lifted it over his head (which is not easy I wouldn't think) and said, "I'm going to kill you." As he started to walk toward me, I flipped over a large plastic see-saw and crawled under it. I began to pray, "Jesus, help me!" He came all the way over to where I could see his feet standing right in front of where I was crouched in terror. He stopped and said nothing more but just stood there a moment. I finally looked up at his face and as it changed back to normal and he put the chair down he said, "Have you seen the pastor's daughter today?" I just stared at him for a moment searching to see if it was a cruel joke and that is when the enemy whispered a thought saying, "I can use them to kill you too." It was not too long after that happened that I became a latch-key kid, staying home while Mom worked. I was not allowed to go outside and no one was allowed to come in the house. During the summers, my cousin and a neighborhood friend were with me quite a bit, but during the school year, I was home alone until my parents got off work.

Death, death, and more death

Later the next year, the pastor's daughter died of cancer. I watched Mom help take care of her the months leading up to her death, getting up at all hours of the night to go and give her shots for pain. She died on Labor Day, 1977 and my grandfather, who also had cancer and lost his vocal chords, one eye, and cheekbone, died in November, 1977.

Then and for the next several years, I would watch my grandmother provide hospice-type care for her husband, mother, father, and half-brother until the day they died. Three of them died in her home. She also cared for her brother until she was not physically able, and he died months later at a nursing care facility. I watched many people die. Looking back, however, it seems that for every bad incident I experienced or was a party to, the Lord would turn things around with a more redemptive perspective. The family members were old and what better place for them to come to the end of life than with family. I know it was hard on my grandmother, but she did it willingly and she did a great job from what I observed.

Positive diversions

In addition to a missionary we housed for a few years and the foster children, we also took in family members, each for a season. One of my distant cousins came with a Saint Bernard who shared equal affection with me as he did my cousin. He always made me feel safe and we took long walks every day. My parents took in wayward kids who Dad would take to work and teach a trade. We even took in an alcoholic who needed to dry out for a bit. In spite of my inner struggles, I loved many of those seasons and through observation and great listening skills, I learned so much about people. It enlarged my heart for ministry.

At church, I think my friends would say that I was pretty normal and outgoing—although we were not a very large group. I felt more comfortable around the Christian friends and families I had grown up with for years. However, in school—which was in a different town and where I attended practically all my life, I was still very quiet except when someone needed prayer or help. Kids at school would slip notes in my school books, confiding in me that they were in trouble and that they wanted prayer. When this happened, it was not uncommon for me to instinctively know how to respond and how to pray for them. I was so strange to everyone for so long, due to the accident as well as being a known Christian, that I did not have a lot of close friends—maybe four.

Here we go again!

When I was thirteen, we traded homes with my aunt and uncle and moved back into Dennis Hollow. I would say that my

Dad spent more time away from home at this time of my life than before. It was around this time that both of my parents were business owners, so they were both gone, sometimes until late at night. I would leave all the doors open. My grandmother, who could look out her front window and see our house, would call me and say, "Monica Ann, why on earth do you have the doors open? Shut those doors until your parents get home." I would say, "No. I cannot do that. If someone comes in the front door, I can run out the back." That was my strategy.

Soon after we moved in, I was stalked by a man for a couple months. As I waited at the end of our long drive for the bus each morning, he would drive up and down the highway watching me. Sometimes, he was parked in an empty area at the end of our property or sitting in my uncle's driveway when I got off the bus in the afternoon. A bit later, I assume that it was he who came to my window at night a few times until I finally told my Dad and he went outside after him in the middle of the night with a shotgun. This really redeemed so many times that my Dad was absent due to work. I needed him to be there for me—to make me feel protected. Seeing how my family would not sit back and take this foolishness made enough impression on that man that I never saw him again. **Sometimes, until you confront evil, it will do as much as you are willing to tolerate.**

Death seemed to find me in all sorts of ways. Serious things were still happening around me. The first boy who showed any interest in me committed suicide. He seemed very nice and attended our youth group, but there were serious issues going on in his life of which we were unaware until he was gone. I was too young to date anyway, so there was little involvement between us, but it was very sad and made me nervous. The next young man who showed interest in me used manipulation by threatening suicide a few times. I finally had nothing more to do with him and prayed that the Lord would protect me from guys like him. I soon met a young man who loved the Lord and was really kind. We were great friends and he was very good to me.

Time to Get Some Grit!

By 1975, mom and dad's lives were still quite busy. My Dad's construction company won the bid to build three Days Inn Motels. He parked our RV on the property of one of the job sites to double as security. The entire family stayed in the RV for half of my school year. The motel was just off the interstate but across from a neighborhood that was mostly African-American families. So the first day of school, I waited for the bus. When I boarded the bus, I know that I must have appeared much whiter as I was the only white girl on the bus—for half of the year! My first day taught me what I was in for—it was quite an experience and very educational in regard to things I had never seen nor heard. I had come to the time and place in my life where I needed to learn how to strategize my own security. For a few days, I watched two girls get on the bus. They were sisters. One was skinny but I heard she could throw good-sized boys across the room if necessary. The other one weighed about 300 pounds and was mentally-challenged. She was one of the kindest girls I had ever met. People also made fun of her, but courage ran in the family and, like her sister, no one messed with her for long. This girl always sat on the front seat of the bus behind the driver. So the next week, when I boarded the bus, I stopped and said, "Can I share this seat with you?" Everyone, including the driver, stopped and waited. Because to share her seat meant that I only had a tiny corner and stuck out a bit in the aisle. But I did not care. She smiled real big and said, "Sure!" Being friends with those girls guaranteed me a bit more protection, which was nice because it was also my first year in high school.

Every day at lunch time, I had to "walk the gauntlet" of a group, including those same bus boys. They always lined the hallway leading to the cafeteria. Between being touched and cat called, it was humiliating and demoralizing.

By my sophomore year I was driving. On the way to school one day, I saw that one of the more popular boys from the "hood" had broken down on the side of the road. So, I stopped and asked if he would like a ride. As he opened the door to get in the car,

I said, "On one condition…" He paused to listen. I said, "I want hallway protection and no more boys bothering me at lunchtime. Otherwise, you can walk." It was quite a ways to school from where we were. He agreed, and I enjoyed peaceful lunchtimes until graduation. I was beginning to come out of my shell.

Their God Becomes My God

I continued to remain faithful to church and my youth group, and started serving God more for myself. That time in my life was that delicate transition between serving the "God of our fathers" as opposed to our own beliefs. The only thing I questioned about my faith was whether or not the "teachings" or rules of the church were really that crucial to my relationship with God.

I soon experienced the Baptism in the Holy Spirit. My gifts grew stronger. I also became increasingly sensitive to any demonic activity around me. I had been singing in church choir and in school for years. It was one thing that always made me feel better. King Saul had a similar experience 1 Samuel 16:23. Any time he felt irritated, he called for a minstrel. Once the music began, he felt comforted and the enemy would leave him alone. I sang every time I had the chance and have been singing every day since I was quite young.

Lurking in the Shadows

Any time we would take school trips to Antebellum houses or any place where the tour guides would say, "This place is haunted" (and a lot of places in Virginia are known for their spiritual activity), I would feel strangely ill and sometimes have to step out of the tour and leave the house. It seems I was surrounded by kids infatuated with witchcraft. My eleventh grade summer school teacher chose to focus our summer school class on the occult, a.k.a. English 11, for four hours every day. I had to take it to skip a year in high school, which I did. However, the juniors did not like it because I left them behind and the seniors did not like it because I was really a junior sharing space with seniors. It was a tough year, but I stayed the course and made it to graduation. I wanted out of school and I wanted out of the area.

Throughout my years in ministry, I have met men and women who were spiritually sensitive as children. As they grew older, they also encountered many opportunities to wander into the New Age or the occult. I have had the privilege of ministering freedom to several people in the body of Christ who, out of spiritual curiosity, the enemy misled into counterfeit experiences. This is just another reason why we must become knowledgeable of Scripture and its warnings about such things. Thankfully, the Lord protected me as I dodged those bullets.

The trap is set

Throughout high school, I was very responsible. I worked and took care of a vehicle. I took my granny on errands and to church, and took care of the house and sometimes prepared meals. I was a good kid, and I thought I was very mature. My parents entrusted me with a great deal of freedom. Many times I traveled with several other kids on road trips to church conferences or Christian concerts, but I was always good about calling home and checking in with Mom.

In the fall of my senior year of high school, my boyfriend of two years had decided to break up because he was in college in another state and was afraid I wanted to get married, which I did. Looking back, I do not blame him. He had not finished his degree and I was only sixteen. I felt the stinging pain of rejection. Jesus can so relate to rejection and it is our responsibility to take it to the cross and lay it down – if we know how. I did not. In spite of my growth, the layers of fear and rejection continued to grow as well. As a result, the enemy was able to set the perfect snare for me at the doorway of transition.

Christmas break of my senior year in high school, I hung out with and grew instantly fond of a young man whom I had known as an acquaintance most of my life. Our families had known each other for many years. He came almost every year from Nashville to visit his grandparents. Nearing the end of the school year, I received a letter from him proposing marriage. I was barely seventeen years old, about to graduate, and feeling like a change of scenery could be helpful. I had become self-confident, not unlike many only children. Therefore, against my father's wishes, I convinced him to allow me to marry. The enemy, who could not nail me through my weaknesses, changed his strategy to target my perceived strength. I remember praying about marrying him, but never listening for an answer. I accepted his proposal and we were married in July, 1980. I knew in my heart the day after we married that I had made a mistake. Receiving no counsel other than to keep the commitment, I left home and moved to Nashville, Tennessee, the wife of a young, talented musician.

Small Town Girl in a Big Town World

My new husband played in the Nashville Symphony. He was also a session musician, for hire in studio recording or with various Music City entertainers. He also played music in church, but our understanding of and relationship with God was different. It was not long after we married that we had a candid conversation about how he was not even thinking of marriage until he met me, and then it was all he could think about. We were both young and somewhat discontent at the time. It was an impulsive decision that we both made, trying to find answers to our discontentment.

My dad came to Tennessee and built a basement apartment in my in-laws' home, where we would live the first three years of our marriage. I spent quite a bit of time with my husband's mom and his younger brother, who was also a year younger than I, and whom I enjoyed very much. I worked and took a few college classes here and there. Within three years, I had worked my way up to a really good position at the University Hospital. I had already been on Valium and was now on Xanax trying to cope with the external stress of being alone many nights and lacking the education to accomplish my dreams. I wanted to be a doctor and that was not going to happen. I was also fighting the internal stress of an immature marriage. More layers of disappointment were thrown onto the pile!

In spite of the desperate choice that took this seventeen year old six hundred thirty-six miles away from home, and in spite of the large pile of unresolved pain in my life, I can testify that the hand of God was on me. I can see where He was very gracious to me. He was more than willing to take all of that from me any time I was willing to yield it to Him. I just did not know how! But I weathered all kinds of dangerous storms in the big city. Looking back, I can see how God mercifully steered me away from things that could have landed me in more trouble than I could have handled.

For all I did not know, I never quit believing that God was able and that He was faithful. One day, I took a step of faith and threw my medication away. I said, "Lord, You are the Healer and You have already been there for me many times before. This is just one more time that I am going to have to trust You. I cannot take this medication and work a job." I remember praying that prayer and throwing my bottle across the room into the trash can and saying, "In the Name of Jesus!" I never took it again after that day.

Warning!

As a counselor, I must say that if you are on prescription medication, "Don't try this at home!" I would NEVER suggest this to anyone. It can be dangerous to quit cold turkey! You should be under the supervision of your physician, who will help you taper off and finally quit taking certain types of prescription medication. You must remember that your body and brain are out of balance and the medication is altering your chemistry to bring it back into balance and keep it there. Do NOT tamper with prescription drugs without the supervision of your doctor. Romans 14:23 says "For whatever does not proceed from faith is sin." If you are not doing something in a place of mountain moving faith and by strong conviction of the Holy Spirit, it is a sin. I am not talking about losing your salvation, but rather how you open doors through which the enemy enters your life to bring destruction.

Sunset of a season

God protected me in my immaturity and He was merciful to me in the measure of faith I had. This protection did not, however, stop the demonic oppression. In spite of the continuing trials, I wanted to be as obedient as I knew how and thus, blessings of continued favor kept coming my way. I still did not know how to yield to or follow His lead. Perhaps I was still too independent. I prayed, but went ahead with my own choices as best I could. I still did not know the Word very well. I had so much shame. I was very insecure about hearing His voice. However, I was still faithful to His house, His people, and the underserved. I was still a good steward with what little I had to manage. All I really knew was the ministry, and that is where I ran to be as close to God as I could. I was a strong witness on the job and I had a close relationship with the various pastors and families who came and went at our little church. It was always my home away from home. Having them in my life brought me comfort but I was not used to anyone probing deeper into my circumstances or my heart. I always seemed to be fine. Whether anyone thought different, I do not know. But they did not ask and I did not offer. This is why we MUST come into closer relationship in the body of Christ. I thank God all the time for the body life that David and I now enjoy at Christian Life Church, where we have been so blessed with safe, intimate friendships for many years.

After six years of marriage, that season came to a close shortly after I experienced a miscarriage with our twins. I remember singing on stage the night before it happened. The Holy Spirit moved in such a powerful way and I felt this amazing sense of peace wash over me. I thought, "Something awesome is about to happen!" By the next morning, I was hemorrhaging. Somehow my peace remained intact, all the way through surgery weeks later. Often, the loss of children becomes the "straw that breaks the camel's back" when that loss is compounded with prior strain on the marriage. Around the time of my due date, I strangely received a congratulations letter from the hospital. It was highly unusual since I never delivered. The letter was the perfect opportunity to put a knife in our hearts. It was only a few months after we received that letter that we filed for a divorce.

In spite of some good times together, our marriage was dying from the day after it began. We limped through. More damage ensued. The twins died. Then the marriage died. That was the sad end of a long story.

After our divorce, I had already left our church in Nashville and found a small Assembly of God church where I was currently residing. There I met a small group of young adults and made some great new friends.

Being a hard worker and open to learning everything vocationally that I could, I had finally worked my way up the ladder to being a Convention Manager at Vanderbilt University Medical Center. I was a career woman, afraid of men and very competitive to survive as a single woman. I still made a few ignorant, dangerous, emotional choices, but the Lord protected me supernaturally, and I knew it. There were many times I asked Him why my life was so hard. Of course, I never heard anything. One thing I never did was blame Him for my circumstances. I wanted to grow. I wanted to make better choices. I was opening my heart for help.

The Conclusion of the Matter

1 John 3:8 states,

"Whoever makes a practice of sinning is of the devil, for the devil has been sinning from the beginning. The reason the Son of God appeared was to destroy the works of the devil."

What I hope can be clearly seen in the relaying of my story thus far is that the works of the devil begin with each person from birth. His strategies for each one may be somewhat different, but his goals are the same:

1) Start weaving a web of lies into the thinking of each person as early as possible and perpetuate those lies through carefully orchestrated events, spoken words, ignorance or neglect, and so on. For those who do not receive Christ (and even some who do) the enemy can either terminate through self-destruction or easily use to carry out hell's destruction on others.

2) For those who receive Christ, his job is to keep them satisfied with salvation alone. Then, he tries to keep them preoccupied with the lies of the painful past and/or the cares of life. This way, believers do not experience mind renewal or healing enough to reach their destiny and become effective for the Kingdom of God and against the kingdom of darkness.

As you continue to read, my hope is that you will:
1) Find Christ if you have not made the decision to receive Him and walk with Him already;
2) Connect the dots of the enemy's work in your own life, to identify the lies by which the enemy is controlling your thoughts, emotions, and actions;
3) See how the hand of the Lord has already been working along the path of your life;
4) Be inspired to become intentional about your healing, training, testing, and the fulfillment of the good works God has called you specifically to do in the earth during your lifetime (Ephesians 2:10).

After all of the bad news, the good news is that together, we can join the Lord in His work, be filled with unspeakable joy, share the Father's love, enforce Christ's victory in the earth, and glorify Him through our obedience to advance the Kingdom!

Chapter Two

Personal Application

1. What are the benefits of telling your story?

_____

_____

2. What are some of the reasons people are afraid to face their story?

_____

_____

3. What was significant about Jacob telling the Lord his name?

_____

_____

4. What are the steps involved in safely telling your story?

Step one:_____

Step two: _____

Step three: _____

Step four: _____

5. Have you ever been emotionally out of bounds? If so, describe which emotions you have allowed to go beyond the boundaries of a rational level.

_____

_____

6. List two things for which you can be grateful to have received or experienced during your formative years.

_____

7. Who can we easily blame for the pain that occurs throughout life?

_____

_____

8. What does Ephesians 6:12 say about this?

_____

_____

9. What will happen until you confront evil in your life?

_____

10. Can you see where God has already taken some of your own childhood struggles and turned them around for your good? Yes No

11. What is one thing that happened to you in your childhood that has inspired you to do something or become something positive in your life today?

_____

_____

12. If you could not answer that question with a positive response, what is one thing that you wish the Lord would redeem for you today?

_____

_____

In Closing

Father, in the Name of Jesus I pray for the readers: those who are inspired to ponder the stories and principles I have shared thus far, and those who have decided to join me on this journey. I ask that You would bless them all as they continue to read. I pray that this chapter has inspired them to take a deeper look into their lives and see where You may have protected them, healed them, or redeemed something that the enemy meant for their destruction. I pray that if they do and if, perhaps, they do not find You in their story, that they would invite you into it now. You are not bound by time, and for that I am truly grateful. You have the awesome ability to change our perspective of historical events. I pray that as their hearts are open to see anything You might show them, that You would touch their hearts and minds with healing that only You can provide and in a way that is far above what they could ever imagine. Keep their hearts open to continue reading and to keep stretching as I know the many times I read things that I could not find the courage or desire to finish. Give more grace where it is needed Abba. I ask this in Jesus' Name. Amen.

Chapter Three

FREEDOM FROM PRIDE & PRESUMPTION

"The worst thing you can do when times are hard for you is not to allow God to do anything for you." Wes Switzer

"Therefore let anyone who thinks that he stands take heed lest he fall" (1 Corinthians 10:12).

Some people are idealistic. They are in denial of their needs or they are enjoying their own journey too much to stop, assess, and refuel. You see idealism quite a bit in pre-marriage and marriage counseling, where at least one of the couple is oblivious to how bad things are in reality.

Some people are stubborn and prideful. They know how bad things are, but find it harder to ask for help. Proverbs 16:18 states that, "Pride goes before destruction and a haughty spirit before a fall." Prideful, sometimes independent people (like me in my twenties), may pray quite a bit, when in reality, they are not truly open to change until they hurt bad enough that they realize there is no other recourse. So they cry out to God for help, and just as mercifully as He was with Israel, God lovingly responds to their humility (James 4:6) with a breakthrough of generous proportion. However, when these people get a little breakthrough or receive a bit of counsel that seems to help, they decide that they are doing well enough to coast for a while on yesterday's breakthrough. The moral of this story is to remain humble and open to help, even when you think you've nailed it! This picture was perfectly illustrated in my next season.

It was 1987. I was twenty-three and recently divorced. Much like the title of the popular children's books by Lemony Snicket, my life up to this time resembled a series of unfortunate events! I understand that only a few of the events mentioned in the first chapter were life-altering. However, I hope you see how the succession of many smaller, but similar things can be set up and used by the enemy, whether or not they follow a larger traumatic event. His intention is to keep us focused on his lies and on ourselves instead of on Christ. He wants us to equate our worth with what happens in our lives and not with whom we really are and whom we will become!

Prayerfully Misguided

The divorce made me feel as if someone had pulled off my arm. Because of the pain, I talked to the Lord even more. Talking to Him more made me feel closer to Him, but also a bit overconfident. I met many people through the years who, like me, boasted of praying all the time, and yet their choices did not reflect the guidance of the Holy Spirit or the Word of God. We need a balance of a thorough knowledge of God through His Word as well as the interaction of the Holy Spirit to be successfully led by the Spirit. This balance is how we learn to distinguish the voice of God from our flesh and the enemy. If we are not careful to operate in the knowledge of the truth and the leading of the Spirit, we can be easily driven by unmet needs into places where we can hurt ourselves and others. My lack of knowledge made me quite gullible, and it showed.

The next few choices I made were regretfully misguided. In fact, I walked right into a trap that had the appearance of a ministry opportunity. If you had questioned me on my decision at the time, I would have responded that I felt like the opportunity was from the Lord. Indeed, it was a ministry opportunity, but the way I handled it made it clear that I was doing it to alleviate my pain as much as to minister. I ended up missing the actual opportunity. The people involved were unchanged, possibly even driven further away from a breakthrough. It was a time when I flew very dangerously close to the flame to learn a hard but valuable lesson.

The poor choices also positioned me in heavier spiritual warfare. I knew I needed to resist the enemy and even tried. What I did not realize was that I was creating the opportunities for a bigger fight! I continued to coast on what little knowledge I possessed, but I was getting weary, and the Lord was about to seize the opportunity to make His next move.

I believe the Lord and my mom were working in agreement on my behalf. I know my mother was praying for me because the Lord's Divine intervention was obvious. He often stepped into my circumstances in unusual ways to grab my attention and steer me out of harm's way. I am thankful for the intercession and how the Lord responds to the prayer of faith. Without my mother's prayers, I probably would have continued heaping insult upon injury, pushing my next breakthrough further down the timeline.

The Wounded Healer

I was definitely more mature than as a girl of seventeen: successful in a career path, traveling around the nation, prospering in ministry, and certainly more empathetic to the needs of others. But I was also less trusting and more determined than ever to take care of myself. I had an appearance of being more confident, but I was much like a wounded animal. Whenever my dog was hit by a car and we went to help him out of the street, he tried to bite us because he was wounded and afraid. That was me. While I looked like I had it together on the outside, if you bumped into my wounds, you saw a different side of me. I was very gifted but easily triggered. Here is the sad news about wounded, gifted people: gifts + wounds + undeveloped character = a huge risk. Your gifts should never take you where a lack of healing and character will not sustain you. If you are truly submitted to God's will and timing, He will never lead you to higher levels of responsibility until your character is ready to bear the weight of that responsibility. He loves you too much to let you get that far because it is not safe! You can run past His roadblocks, but they will always be there to stop you if you heed them. If you are not sensitive to His voice or His prompting, you may not see or recognize them. Many times people go where they want and as far as they want whether God is opening the door or not—even in the ministry. What is worse is that those in authority who are desperate for help will often put people who are not prepared into positions of leadership.

Going to Another Level

When I got involved in a little Assembly of God church, I loved my new group of friends; one of them in particular. It was not because I was looking for someone to date; I was too fresh out of the lawyer's office! But I was attracted to him because of his passion for the Lord. He had something I wanted to cultivate more in my own life. He was the unofficial head of the group since he was older than anyone else, but I began to admire him for many reasons: he was a recent college graduate, worshipped freely, and was kind and gentle. He had no agenda, which made him a safe friend to have at a very crucial time.

One day, he challenged our little group to fast and pray and to seek the Lord for the "next right thing" we should do in our lives. He was ready for a wife himself, but he wanted God's choice. He had a list of what he would like in a woman, but he was choosing to lay it on the altar and fast and pray with an open heart just like everyone else.

I eagerly accepted his challenge! I was ready to answer the call to missions and move to Africa if God would but call me. I was very serious, but I am also certain that I was trying to redeem my life from the bad choice I had made. I had no idea what the Lord's will was for me. But, I was an only child, my husband was gone and my children were in heaven. I had nothing left to hold me back. I knew that if God would call me, I would sell everything and do whatever I had to do to prepare and move in that direction. But, like everyone in our group, I was also willing to put that desire on the altar. Now was the time to slow down and really open my heart to that "next right thing" for me. The question was this: Could I hear Him?

God's Unexpected Answer

I began my fast. I prayed for myself as well as the others and the things we were all laying on the altar. I fasted and prayed on and off for several weeks and into the next month. During that time, the more I would pray, something unexpected kept coming to the forefront of my mind. It would also well up in my heart. I tried to rebuke it several times. I thought it was the devil trying to distract me. I literally fought it. Then I refocused and continued to pray. I started dreaming about it. Continuing to pray, I found myself distracted by it at work. Thoughts about it kept me from falling asleep some nights. But how on earth could it be true? So one day I said, "This is ridiculous! I'm going to do something about this. It is either God, or it has to stop!" So I called the only guy I trusted to steer me right.

On the other side of town, this young man was washing his dishes. He had eclectic tastes for a man of twenty-seven. He was enjoying the "easy listening" radio station–you know the kind that plays instrumental music from the old movie era? So, there he was washing his dishes and the song "Somewhere My Love" was playing. The tune played, "Some-where my love…" and the phone rang at the exact moment he sang that line. He heard the phone ring, pointed to the phone and said, "And there she is!"

So he picked up the phone, and I was on the other end saying, "David, do you have a minute? I have been faithfully doing this fast, and I think something is either wrong, or I am hearing God and it is not at all what I expected. Can I come and talk to you about it this evening after church?"

He said, "Certainly." Good ole' Dave!

We met at church as usual. After service, I followed him to his apartment. I had never been there before. I had a home and usually hosted our group there, or we would meet for dinner at a local restaurant. I followed him through the door of his apartment and distinctly remember the temperature almost took my breath. But after all, he was very thin. He had a skinny woman on his wish list too. I do not remember one skinny day in my life! I would say that, even back then, I had fluffy curves, and the heat in that apartment was overwhelming for me! That added a bit of tension to my topic for the evening.

Once inside, I noticed that he had a mural of a surfer on his wall, a large fish tank in the corner, and a fish net on the opposite wall. I pushed my eyebrow back down. Then I asked to use his restroom and, don't ask me why I was so nosey, but I opened his linen closet and there was a picture of a parrot on the wall inside. (I am literally crying with laughter as I write this!) I thought, "Oh my."

I came back into the living room where he was calmly seated. I was thinking about what a great guy he was. He was very sweet—at least as far as I knew. He had kissed dating goodbye for the last two years to write thoughts about God and to grow spiritually. I thought that was just the coolest thing! I had only known him for about six months. So there I sat smiling and nervously wondering how to start this conversation as I was rubbing my hand across his couch. That is when I noticed the rattan furniture we were sitting on. "Hmmm."

Finally, using the most confident, only child, straight-to-the-point, spit-it-out and get-it-over-with tone, I said, "Dave, I have been fasting and praying—very faithfully. At first, I thought I was under attack so I rebuked the devil and prayed harder. But then, the harder I prayed, the more I kept seeing this one thing over and over and over again. I have never really waited on God or had this experience before. But I want His will so much right now and I must be sure that I am doing this right! Sometimes I cannot sleep for thinking about what I THINK He is showing me. Then, it pops into my mind at work and I have a hard time concentrating. I rebuke it and it comes right back! I have cried out to the Lord to make it stop if it is just me, but how can I know for sure? Lately I began to wonder if it WAS God?"

So he asked, in his so-gentle-you-almost-cannot-hear-him voice, "Well? What on earth is it?"

And I said, "Every day as I have prayed for God to reveal His will for my life, I only see one thing." By this time, my eyes were very wide as I looked at him. I am sure by this moment that there was the gassiest look on my face!

He said, "And...?"

I said quietly, "It's you." I braced myself for a gentle, but certain rebuke; but I wanted to know the truth, and I was hungry and wanted to move on and get something to eat.

I never took my eyes off of him after I said it. He paused a moment, crossed his legs the other direction and said, "Well, that is perplexing." While I was searching for a definition, he went on to say, "...because I have been thinking the same thing about you for the last two weeks as I have prayed."

I am certain that I cocked my head a bit sideways. I said, "Are you kidding?"

He shook his head, "No."

Suddenly, a sweet, little smile slid onto my lips and I said, "Oh really? So what should we do about this?"

He said, "You want to go out tomorrow evening?"

I said, "Sure!" So he walked me to my car. I got in and he shut my door. I turned around in my seat and watched my mission field walk back to the sweltering beach house. That was February 25, 1987.

Close Encounter of the Prophetic Kind

The next several months we saw each other every day. David actually asked the Holy Spirit how to date me and what I liked. I know he heard the Lord because it was the most fun I'd had in a long time. God rewards those who diligently seek Him (Hebrews 11:6). Actually, the season was redemptive for both of us. Prior to the two years David had dedicated to the Lord, he had been in a couple of unhealthy relationships as well.

Shortly after that, I was in a public place. There was a woman in town that I did not know well. She was only an acquaintance. She was struggling with depression and often times, she was almost not there, probably from medication. This woman, however, was like me in that God often worked through her in spite of her battle. I could see it, and one day I experienced it. This particular day was one of those days when I could tell that she was present in body, but very numb. I never had a conversation with her. I didn't even see her that often. But this day, she was with me among a crowd. We were not even standing closely at all. In fact, she was quite a ways away when I saw her and she saw me and her eyes locked on me as if to say, "I'm coming after you!"

I was suddenly paralyzed, more out of curiosity of what was about to happen, because I was strangely not afraid of her. She walked through the crowd, coming toward me. I just stood there. She kept coming. I kept my eye on her. Finally she walked right up to me and took my chin in her hand. Standing very close so that I could hear her softly speaking, she looked me straight in the eyes. She was suddenly NOT medicated. Her eyes went from weak to soft but very intentional, and she said, "Honey, the Lord loves you. He knows exactly where you've been and what you've been through. He saw everything. You keep following Him because one day, He is going to impact a lot of people through your life and He wanted you to know that."

Then her eyes turned weak again, she smiled and let go of my face, dropping her hand as if it weighed a thousand pounds. She walked right past me and into the crowd as if I were not even there. I stood frozen for a bit because I had never experienced that before. But it definitely made an impression on me: one that I will never forget!

In fact, there is a scene in the movie *God's Not Dead*. Near the end of the movie, this selfish, rich young man finally visits his mother, who has a severe case of Alzheimer's. He is airing his agnostic opinion where he compares his wicked, successful life to her faithful, pathetic life. Suddenly his mother has this unbelievably lucid moment where she speaks the wisdom of God to her son about his prison cell of unbelief. As soon as the Lord is done speaking through her, she turns to him and says, "Who did you say you were again?" It was just like that!

The Fairy Tale Begins

Around April, I received a piece of mail at work. It was from David. I opened it and it was just one piece of paper. My eyes got really wide and I laughed and laughed with joy. It was David's list with the attributes of the woman he wanted to marry. He had drawn one of those circles with a line through it and wrote in big red letters out to the side, "I CHOOSE YOU!" This was huge! I was accepted! Things were really looking up for me!

In May of that year, David took me to the hotel where I often worked managing conferences. Not knowing anything about his plans for the evening, I suggested that we enter the hotel through a back entrance where the parking was easier. He did not want to spill the beans about his surprise, so he played along like it was not a big deal. But in the next few minutes, we both got an even bigger surprise! As we walked up this grand staircase to the back entrance, we noticed a gorgeous blonde man dressed in a white tuxedo and holding a violin in his hand. I thought David knew him. The man was smiling this big, gentle smile, as if he knew us. That smile was like a tractor beam, so we walked right up and stood in front of him. He bowed and placed the violin to his chin and began to play, "Some-where My Love…" I know my mouth was hanging open like a carp. We listened to the entire song. He finished, bowed again and smiled. We thanked him and climbed the few remaining stairs to the portico door of the hotel. As we walked,

I said, "Oh Dave! That was so romantic. He played our song. Where did you find that guy?"

He stopped while turning around and said, "I thought you knew him!" It had been less than a minute when we turned to get a second look at him and he was gone! He vanished into thin air—violin in tow! If you're hearing the theme to *The Twilight Zone* right now, or even better, angels singing, "Aaaahhhhh!" I think you're on the right track! That is, at least, what we believe. Dave had planned many surprises for the evening, but God trumped his efforts with a miracle!

It was an amazing night. He walked me through the plant-filled Conservatory, stopping at waterfalls and the gazebo to read several poems he had written for me. He walked me to another spot and said something that matched the theme of where we were standing. Then he walked me to a gift shop and compared me to something precious and valuable. Then he walked me back to the conservatory. By this time, the angels were not singing any longer. I had on four inch heels and this girl was tired and ready to sit down!

The Conservatory was absolutely packed! There was some kind of ball going on in the hotel, and it was swarming with men and women all decked out for the occasion. I looked around and there was nowhere to sit except for a small table with two chairs just inside the roped off area where the harpist was playing. The table was so close to where the harpist played that it was almost under his nose! While it was unusual for me to waltz into a crowd and do anything, I could not resist the opportunity to sit down; so I grabbed Dave's hand and practically dragged him over the ropes and into the private area where harpist was playing. We sat down—right under his nose!

David seemed strangely calm in light of my brave, yet brazen response to fatigue. I started getting a bit nervous but decided to focus on the show. Strangely, no one else seemed to care about our little intrusion either. I kept my eyes glued on the harpist, my palms getting a bit sweaty. He did a wonderful show as usual. This night, however, he did something I had never seen before. He put his larger harp aside, and while he spoke about the privilege of participating in weddings at the hotel, a young man brought out a solid emerald miniature harp. It was exquisite and just happened to be my birthstone, so I was mesmerized. I think my hands were trembling by this time. He placed the harp on our table and, to my amazement; he began to play, "Amazing Grace." I had never heard him play a hymn in the show, but after all, this was no ordinary night! I was almost in tears by that time. I could feel a lump in my throat so large that I wondered if anyone could actually see it.

When the harpist was finished playing the song, he talked about how he often met really special people and how he was so glad to see one of them there that night. He said, "My new friend Dave and I get to do something really special here tonight." I thought I would slide right under the table! He pulled a ring box out of his bejeweled jacket, popped it open and looked me straight in the eyes and said, "Monica Ann Lambert... will you accept David Robertson's hand in marriage?"

I do not remember, now twenty-seven years later, how I got it out, but somehow I managed to squeak out a faint "Yes." The crowd erupted in applause. I looked around and there were even more people than when I had made a mad dash for that table. Cameras began to flash like the paparazzi and people began to call out to us, "Way to go! That was beautiful!"

We were the stars of the show that evening, and when it ended, we got up to leave after a kiss for the crowd. As we walked through the hotel to go to the car, people were still calling out to us as if we were celebrities. "Dave! That was awesome," one couple said. It was magical.

We exited the building and reached the car. It happened to be the day before my 24th birthday. Dave had a gift for me. I opened the package and it was a beautiful watch. The little winding pin was popped out and as I went to pop it back in, I said, "Look Dave!" It was the exact time of the moment I popped it in without having to set the watch. I said, "Can this night get any more strange and wonderful?" We thanked the Lord for the evening and headed back to Murfreesboro.

I told you that story because, I love to tell it and do not get the chance to do so very often. We were featured in the *Nashville Banner* and the *Tennessean* and invited to be guests on *The Talk of the Town* morning show.

Finally, the day came when we were to be wed – July 4, 1987. I had planned a very inexpensive wedding, but it was simply elegant. Dave did the coolest thing to start the ceremony. He had everyone stand and give applause to our Guest of Honor – the Holy Spirit – whom he publicly credited for bringing us together. Then the musical group I was in sang a song that says, "He is here – let's celebrate the Presence of the Lord." Then I sang to David and he played a special song for me. It was such a great day! We laughed and had a great time with our dearest friends, family, and co-workers.

We did it! We were husband and wife! We honored and obeyed the Lord! We sought the Lord and waited for help, and I thought I had nailed this! We both did. But what happened next was not what either of us had expected.

Prepare for Marriage before You Pass "Go!"

Looking back and speaking as a counselor, I want to say that for as much as we were in love, as much as we talked, and as much as we knew that we were walking in the will of God in our courtship, we still needed pre-marital counseling. To be honest, however, we were not very close to the pastor, and he resigned the church months before we married. We knew of no one at the time who was a counselor, and I had never heard of pre-marital counseling back then. God knew this and He had a plan in spite of it all. I say all of this to make a strong point! I would NEVER suggest for any couple to marry without a solid, biblical pre-marriage counseling regimen and one that includes a foundation of assessing compatibility (not to judge it but improve it), unpacking life-changing life experiences, and healing old wounds. Follow that up with a strong education about faith, communication and conflict, differences, needs, roles, sex, money, children and so on. If it is available, and it is today more than ever, pre-marital counseling is vitally important and you will see why as you keep reading.

The Tale Darkens

First, I knew by the events of our honeymoon that something was amiss. Suddenly, it was like something had blocked the heavens, and where we had experienced great favor and ease for months, things were now quite different. Although we enjoyed beautiful fireworks against the night sky almost the entire way to Miami, several unusual things happened once we arrived.

No one spoke English – or sign language – or even hand jive – at the airport! The limo David had arranged was nowhere to be found for quite some time. Hello aggravation. The next day, we visited a nearby zoo. By taxi, it cost us $45 to get there. Hello disappointment. Then, we were eaten up to our thighs by sand fleas by the time we left. Hello misery.

We took a subway back for fifty cents each –yea! But got off a couple blocks too soon – boo! We ended up in a seedy part of town, a bit too far from the hotel, but thought we would walk the rest of the way back. We prayed in tongues as we calmly, but quickly, walked through the area. Thankfully, we made it back with our worldly goods and our lives. Hello fear. I am slowly starting to lose confidence in this man's ability to protect me! Hello insecurity.

The next day, still itching, we boarded our cruise ship and realized that we were there among two graduating senior classes. I have never seen so much white lipstick in all my life! I saw this one young girl staring at Dave – as I was sitting on his lap. It would be difficult, if not impossible, NOT to know he was "with someone." Hello lust.

When we got to our cabin, there was a message on our phone. Little Miss White Lips had mysteriously found our room number and left a message asking David if he wanted to meet her for a drink. Everywhere we went after that, if I saw any of those kids, I had my eye on every girl to see who had her eyes on David. Hello jealousy and suspicion. I would have been livid over the unexpected proposition if I were not already seething over the fact that the woman, who booked our cabin back at the travel agency in our city, gave us a room with TWIN BEDS! It turns out she wanted to marry David herself! Hello unforgiveness. But that is not the worst part.

Halfway through our honeymoon, we boarded a tinder boat and went to this little island to go snorkeling. David was under water taking in the beauty of the incredibly colorful creatures. I was under water chasing a cute little fish that kept darting away just as I was about to grab his tail – as I am the whisperer of animal, fish, and fowl. So to propel myself faster, I grabbed what I thought was a piece of coral and it turned out to be one of those weird, spikey fishes that emit poison to predators like me! I came up and out of the water, grasping my hand and screaming! Dave jumped up as well and looked at my hand while I continued to scream! It was so painful, and you could see the poison traveling up my arm. Hello death and destruction! We were literally in the lagoon of *Gilligan's Island*, and it dawned on Dave to do the only thing there was to do! He laid hands on me and prayed for healing in the Name of Jesus. Suddenly, my hand stopped hurting, and when we looked, the poison was gone and I was fine. Whew! Hello faith! What a roller coaster ride this was, and those are just the highlights!

Stop Coasting and Start Praying – This is War!

Finally, we stopped coasting and started praying together! Sound familiar? Presuming we had taken the hill, we thought we could coast down the other side, which is what a lot of people do. Our humility only lasted as long as we were desperate. Once we had heard the Lord and obeyed, we thought we had it made and life would be relatively easy!

The rest of the cruise continued to be a comedy of errors, but it was minimal by comparison to the first few days of the honeymoon. We went on to have a good time together and we finally made it home safe and sound.

We were completely blindsided by this sudden difficulty after such a peaceful courtship and engagement. It was as though the enemy said, "You and me—It's ON!"

I was accustomed to struggling, but I thought this was turning over a new leaf! We were in God's will! Why the OBVIOUS warfare? God had protected me from errors in judgment before. This was a whole new level of warfare!

First, it WAS another level of warfare. New level—new devil! In my mind, I can see a scene. The Holy Spirit is leading us, like children, into a new territory. We are following behind Him, and before we go across the threshold into the new territory, He says, "Stay behind Me." Why? It is because He knows that if we could see in the spiritual realm, there are still targets painted on us. Yes, we are obedient by accepting the mission, but we are carrying unresolved issues into the mission with us. If we walk in the Spirit—staying in step behind Him, He can warn us and even protect us. Protect us from what? There is an air assault seeking to destroy us, and it is watching for those targets of rejection, fear, jealousy, and so on. These are all targets the enemy can see very clearly; doors of access through which the enemy can drop bombs to attack us. But we, in our presumption look at each other and say, "So what! He is WITH us!" We presumptuously come out from behind Him and start running through the field, innocently squealing, "Wheeeeeee!" Then suddenly, "POW! BANG!"

"How is that fair?" you might ask yourself. It makes no difference to the enemy if he legally gets at you due to your willful sin or lie-containing wounds, or if he illegally attacks you because you are trying to step into territory upon which he has a claim. If you have not removed your targets or you do not know how, find help or stay off the battlefield.

Marriage is one of those territories to which the enemy has laid claim. Why? It is because marriage is SUPPOSED to tell the truth about God—one man, one woman, walking with God—a three-fold cord (Ecclesiastes 4:9-12; Ephesians 5:32). Dave Harvey, in *The Art of Marriage: Getting to the Heart of God's Design* states, "Marriage is embedded in the culture as a gospel testimony that is always making statements. The only question is whether it's a good statement or a bad one."[1] If you look around today, the enemy has definitely staked his claim in marriage. His activity in marriage is rampant, and our lack of knowledge makes his job simple (Hosea 4:6). God made men and women grossly different, from brain biology to needs to anatomy, so that no one gets to remain selfish! Marriage is miserable for selfish people because one of the targets is the sin of selfishness!

Now, take all that is naturally challenging in marriage and throw some spiritual warfare on top of it all! That is where we were. We presumptuously thought that one act of obedience was going to make everything okay, when in reality, our unresolved issues could be triggered by a composite of little things. It did not take much to set us off.

The Lord most definitely led us to marry. However, we were blind-sided by what this marriage would draw out of us. Our past and our independence were no problem as long as we were not sharing space or trying to work together as a team. However, once we were living together and had to consider someone else's needs, disappointments from past relationships and selfish independence quickly manifested. We loved each other, but each day was a battle to see who would get their needs met first.

The Blame Game

During the first several months of marriage, we were quick to point fingers at each other. Hello blame-shifting. Then we tried to change each other. Suddenly, David wanted me to become like the woman on that list! I was only a few out of the ten things he had listed in the first place, and that was only because I was a spirit-filled believer and I dyed my hair! Hello betrayal! We were not responding to each other the same way we had been brought together: by walking in the Spirit. No! We were REACTING to each other in the flesh! Pride and selfishness, both common discoveries in the newness of marriage, were being exposed in us. We both had a strong will and neither of us wanted to give much.

On the surface, we looked just fine. "Hello Brother Robertson, Sister Robertson. How are you tonight?" "We are doing great! And you?" Our "stuff" was hiding in the locked rooms of our soul. Just as you never know what kind of juice is in an orange until you squeeze it–likewise, you never really know what is in the depths of your soul until you are faced with just the right amount of pressure to S-Q-U-E-E-Z-E it out. I was just the right amount of pressure for David, and he was the same for me. God knew it, and He was about to start using it for our good. He would use our differences to become the sand paper that would smooth out many rough edges! And He would use our ignorance in marriage to drive me exactly where I was longing to go–deeper!

We had so much to learn. However, as challenging as the relationship had become, we kept coming back to the fact that we were "called" to walk together. Out of desperation to please God, our commitment to him remained our first priority. On a positive note, we rode our bicycles every morning to the MTSU campus where we would stop, read a Bible passage or a devotional together and pray. It was through this daily altar time that we felt encouraged to hang in there, to trust God, and to serve others, even if we had yet to feel comfortable serving each other.

What the Enemy Means for Destruction, God Uses for Good

So far, in our story, you have seen two spiritual dynamics working in tandem in this chapter. You have seen the intense spiritual warfare that is leveraged against those who may have "fire insurance" but have not learned to surrender their unresolved pain to Christ. First Timothy 6:12 commands us to "fight the good fight of faith." Second Corinthians 10:4 describes the weapons of our warfare. We are in a war, and when you are wounded, you do not remain on the battlefield–you go to triage. But while that battle is raging, you are also in the hands of a redemptive God who, "...causes everything to work together for the good of those who love God and are called according to his purpose for them" (Romans 8:28 NLT).

In the days ahead, God would take our desperate need for deliverance and use it to fashion our destiny, as He is very resourceful and wastes nothing! For the time being, however, our fairy tale turned soap opera very quickly. Our expectations were WAY higher than either of us could deliver.

We were a bit of a mess! But even still, God had us in the palm of His hand. Being in a mess is many times how a coaching or counseling relationship ensues. We were hurting, but we were not hurting badly enough yet! I was a revolving door of unmet needs, and the enemy still had plenty of access to my life. I needed a deeper relationship with the Lord, I needed healing, and I needed a better relationship with my husband. Remembering the fasting and prayer that brought me to this difficult season, I remembered that in the time of consecration, I had availed myself to God for a mission. I thought I could skip the training since I did not get called to a foreign country. Since He revealed this WAS my mission, I warmed up to the idea of walking beyond what I had always known. The Lord was preparing my heart for higher education!

By the way, I let him enjoy that rattan furniture for about four years before I finally convinced him to let me sell it. We enjoyed a beautiful blue sectional for the next twenty years. ☺

Chapter Three

Personal Application

1. Check which one of the two types of people mentioned in the opening of this chapter which described you at some point in your life?
   ☐ Idealistic   ☐ Stubborn and prideful

2. Describe a time in your life when you had a moment of surrender. Perhaps it was after the death of a season when, like me, you cried out from the ash heap and God opened a door to a fresh, new season.

_____

_____

3. After a fresh, new season, when you are enjoying a spiritual high, have you ever presumed to be doing so well that you stopped doing the disciplines and started coasting on yesterday's victory? What happened as a result of your experience?

_____

_____

4. Think of an example of how the enemy attacked you because of willful sin. Then write another example of when he attacked you for trying to grow spiritually or advancing into one of his claimed territories.
   a) _____

_____
   b) _____

_____

5. What people or circumstances do you remember that turned out to be the "right pressure" to unveil your unresolved issues?

Freedom from Pride & Presumption

What were those issues? Did you resolve them and if so, how did you resolve them?

_____

_____

6. What two spiritual dynamics are often at work simultaneously throughout life?
a) _____

_____

b) _____

_____

7. Describe a season in your life when you were under attack but, look back and see where God was protecting you, or where He turned things around for your good?

_____

_____

8. Are you the type of person that gets help because you want it, or do you wait until you hurt badly enough or get in trouble to find it? If you reported the latter, how do you feel about that at this stage of your life, and is it something you would consider changing if you could?

_____

_____

9. What spoke to you the most from this chapter and what is a "next right step" for you in regard to what the Coach may be speaking to you as a result of what you read?

_____

_____

In closing...

Father, in the Name of Jesus, we worship You. We love you, and we are thankful that you make ALL things work together for our good. In the midst of bad things, regardless of whether they were invited by sinful choices or an attack against our vulnerability; you are turning it ALL around for our good as that is Your promise. We choose to be grateful and thankful for those You have allowed to squeeze us so that nothing inside can remain hidden, for in this way You rescue us from ourselves and from the hand of the enemy. We honor the creativity of Your provision. You are so resourceful with our days; You do not waste anything. We ask for eyes of redemption as we continue to examine ourselves. Do not allow us to look at certain events as being beyond Your reach. In humility, strengthen us to surrender the most difficult things to You. For You are committed to our healing. It has been purchased and paid in full! For this we are truly thankful. Amen.

Chapter Four

FROM RELIGION TO RELATIONSHIP

"Now may the God of peace himself sanctify you completely, and may your whole spirit and soul and body be kept blameless at the coming of our Lord Jesus Christ" (1 Thessalonians 5:23).

The core value of commitment in our culture is often very weak. We tend to start well, but we do not necessarily finish well. Commitment to anything takes effort, and many times we would rather stay busy or get busy in everything besides what requires the engaging of our whole self. Commitments usually require us to be "all in" so that we are able to finish strong.

Proverbs 25:28 states that "He that hath no rule over his own spirit is like a city that is broken down, and without walls."

In commitments, our spirit must be engaged. The spirit must be the supervisor over the soul and the body. Our spirits must be yielded to the spiritual fruit of self-control. If not, chances are that, unless we are motivated by some desire of the flesh, such as greed or the esteem of man, we may very well lose interest and give up on our commitments.

In commitments, our souls must be engaged. Your soul is second in command over your body. Under the supervision of our spirits, our minds, will, and emotions must be on board with our commitment. You must be thinking about the goals of your commitment, the cost of your commitment, and the ultimate rewards of your commitment. As you think these thoughts, certain emotions will follow. If you want to experience pleasant emotions, you must cast down the thoughts that will come to dissuade you from what you wish to accomplish.

In commitments, our bodies body must be engaged. As you are thinking the thoughts that will properly motivate you towards what activities your commitment requires, your body must submit to function to that end. Your commitment may require you to get up early, to eat a certain way, or to fast something for a period of time.

Matthew 26:41 records a conversation between the Lord and His disciples in regard to watching with Him in prayer in the garden of Gethsemane. He said to them, "The spirit is willing, but the flesh is weak." Most of the time, the flesh will resist the commitments you make. That is when your spirit must rise up and say, "Come on! We are doing this today!" Then you engage your mind, will, and emotions accordingly, taking care to not murmur or complain. It is important to keep a good perspective by saying, "I GET to do this," not, "I HAVE to do this."

Fully committed to self and others

With the many modern conveniences available to us today, we are still busy! Most people have too much on their schedule and have no extra time left for emergencies, relaxation, recreation, meaningful conversation, or conversational prayer (where we are talking and listening to God). In our busy schedules, the most important things that NEED to get done are often the things that get pushed to the wayside. This is a dangerous pitfall because it usually means we are taking care of everything and everyone except ourselves. I am not talking about selfish-care, but true self-care: things that are essential to our physical and spiritual health and mental/emotional development.

In order to flourish, our spiritual lives and relationships require commitment. We must be "all in." If we do not fully engage the spirit, soul, and body in our spiritual lives and in our relationships, particularly in marriage, we will fall into a religious rut where we are trying to exact our self-worth out of being dutiful. We might go through the motions, but lack the enjoyable emotions that should accompany healthy intimacy. What we do might become so ritualistic that we find other ways to stay busy and merely do the least required to "hang on" for as long as possible. Honestly, it is often times easier to hang on as relationships, and marriages in particular, only work when you work at them. A spiritual relationship, in lieu of dead religious practices, requires dying to your flesh daily, surrendering your brokenness, and being mindful of the Lord's abiding presence. It is honestly easier to become preoccupied with the busyness of our culture and tell ourselves that we are doing well – until we eventually unravel and someone implodes.

One More Night with the Frogs

One of the preachers we served years ago preached a sermon entitled, "One More Night with the Frogs." His scripture passage was taken from Exodus, Chapter 8. God had smitten the land of Egypt with a plague of frogs. They were everywhere and people were miserable. Pharoah called for Moses and begged him to ask God to take away the frogs. Moses asked Pharoah, "When would you like for me to plead with God to take the frogs from among you" [paraphrasing]. Pharoah said, "TOMORROW!" Can you believe it?! Why on earth would he not ask Moses to pray that they would be taken away that very day? More importantly, why do we wait until tomorrow to surrender to God?

In the formative years of our marriage, I was still not ready to surrender, but I was well on my way to being pushed off of the line. I was dancing on the line between falling apart on my own or falling apart in the Lord's arms. God would continue to use my circumstances to push me through the bottle neck. I needed another breakthrough just to get started. Like many, when I saw the effort that it would require to move forward, I became discouraged, dug my heels in and would not move. Thankfully, God had me hemmed in. The enemy was still chasing me, so I did not want to go back. God was going before me, but I was still comfortable with a safe distance between us. He probably had angels, like bouncers, on either side of me so that I could not "cut and run." Where it concerned intimacy with Him, I would continue to be content with baby steps. Where it concerned intimacy with David, suffice it to say that he nicknamed me "The Feminazi." The closer I tried to get to him, circumstances would pop up, making it more of a challenge. The thought of surrendering to his love made me uncomfortable. I wanted to do it, but I was starting to face my fear of vulnerability with men.

First Step of Submission

Shortly before we married, and because we were going to get married, I had given up a recent opportunity to start traveling internationally with my job at Vanderbilt. Then, because we were newlyweds, I also gave up managing conferences in other parts of the nation to take only the ones held on campus. Now, David wanted me to quit the job I loved and come to work with him at his brother's new business. So I did. It was my first BIG sacrifice: my effort to submit to my husband.

David was about to take a buy-out after ten years of service with Kroger. The administrative position with his brother's company would be a great change and a step up for him. Because his college degree was so generic, anyone could see that this job opportunity would give him more experience in another field of employment. With me quitting my job in Nashville and coming to work with him, we would have more time together!

On many occasions, our new jobs were enjoyable and a great way for me to get to know the family. However, the nature of that particular business, as well as the challenges of working with family, raised our stress level to new heights!

Nuclear Reactions

Like most struggling marriages in the early years, not all days were bad. Many of our days were peppered with times of laughter and opportunities to redeem how we felt about ourselves by blessing or serving others. Blessing and serving people can always make bad times more bearable. There is an alternative however. You can also handle how you feel about yourself by putting someone else down. We did our fair share of both.

Some couples come into a marriage carrying the same burden of unresolved trauma, injustice, or the residue of sinful choices from their lives before marriage. Unresolved issues such as these can breed a host of underlying emotions that will eventually mask themselves as anger.

Anything that is hiding inside the soul of an individual, whose stress level becomes oppressive, usually comes to the surface. I call it "soul scum." These times are the perfect opportunity to cry out to God for mercy, to seek comfort from His Word, and receive the help and healing we need in the moment. But, many times, what do we do? Run to find a new distraction!

For David, the distraction was sound ministry. For me, the distraction was volunteering as a youth pastor. We loved our new positions of ministry, and it was not wrong to volunteer for these positions. People were blessed by them. We were blessed by them. We tolerated our jobs, and it was relief of the stress in both the jobs and in our marriage. We were fairly good at controlling ourselves in and among the body, although others may disagree. However, some are not so good at it and tend to express their inner workings to those they serve. This is another reason why we do not need to delay in pursuing any healing that we need.

As for the unresolved issues hiding in our souls, they began to manifest in our home. I was missing my old job and regretful that I gave it up. Although our families are very close now, at the time, he was dealing with generational patterns that became glaringly obvious with all of the family working together. We had many disagreements. Disagreements turned into full-on arguments. We rarely finished an argument because, like most men, David would get emotionally "flooded" and he would leave because I would not shut up. I had been too quiet for most of my life. I was ready to be heard.

I remember one time he became angry and took off on his motorcycle. It was raining. Nothing made me angrier than when he took off in the middle of an argument. When he left, he would not tell me where he was going, which was really bad because he had an eye disease and only 20% of his peripheral vision at the time. It hurt my feelings. It was meant to hurt my feelings. By then, however, I was used to it and knew how to stop my feelings and move on emotionally to spare unnecessary anxiety. I had become tough. I remember thinking, "Whatever!" Then I also remember praying for his safety, probably something such as, "Lord. I know he is being stupid, but thank You for not letting him have an accident and die." That prayer would be the "unsanctified" version of Philippians 4:6.

He came back hours later. He had driven to Fall Creek Falls, and it was dark by the time he returned. Because he was so thin and it was cold and rainy, he had caught a chill.

During the night, I woke up to the most awful moaning. I sat up and David was crawling and rolling around on the floor. I asked him what was wrong and he said that his stomach was hurting really badly. I got dressed and took him to the emergency room. They took a culture (smile) and found that he had picked up a parasite. Poor guy, he had to starve the little critter. They instructed him not to eat anything for three days. He could only drink to remain hydrated. The parasite finally died, and his pain subsided. I was glad he was well. I actually felt a little compassion for his pain. I did not say it, but at the same time, I was thinking, "That'll teach you!"

I cannot stress to you how much better it would be if we could all deal with our pain in the moments following its inception. Having the knowledge, the tools, and the level of relationship we need with Christ in order to find that resolution is what I love to give people today. If I only knew then what I know now!

Prophetic Intercession

Neither of us wanted to have any children. Can you imagine? We were far from ready to raise children. However, during this season, I distinctly remember praying, "Lord, please start healing me now, before I bring children into this world. I don't know when we will have them, but I do not want to pass this pain on to my kids." Without hesitation, I believe that prayer is what made the deepest, most volatile struggles come to the surface. God was answering my prayer as He continued to draw my pain to the surface through circumstances. I could blame the devil, and he had certainly not retired. In fact, he was watching us closely for sinful anger because he knew he had a legal right to attack us when it occurred (Ephesians 4:26). But, I know for a fact that God was using my pain to lead me to the cross for another round of healing. For as much as I wanted to be free, I still resisted. I was desperate to remain in control, and of course, the root of control is fear.

Punching Bag Anyone?

We had no communication tools. We did not run to the bookstore and purchase a copy of *Anger Management for Dummies*. We did not take the time to search the Scriptures for any guidance on how to survive in the midst of emotional chaos. We were "you and me." We could not fathom being "one." I needed him to cover me, to protect me, and to help heal me. I had no idea he was as emotionally broken inside as well. We were a bundle of emotions, but the easiest one to identify and manifest was anger. We were not the type to hurt each other physically, so we began to take our anger out on the walls and furniture. Dad had to come and patch a hole that David punched in the apartment wall. Then he had to come back over and patch a hole I kicked in the apartment wall. I did not want to have the embarrassment of having him come over and fix another hole, so I started kicking other things instead.

I stopped hitting and kicking things the day I kicked a heavy metal desk. I jammed and almost broke my toe, and it really taught me a lesson. David, on the other hand, threw things: big things like bicycles and chairs. He turned over tables. Similarly, he learned his lesson the day he was going to smack a Mylar balloon to emphasize his point! There he sat on the floor. We were very engaged in a disagreement. The balloon was lying next to him on the floor. Even when Mylar balloons are deflated, you cannot tell. In a fit of anger, you do not think about such things. He SMACKED the balloon as hard as he could to make his point! When he did, he actually smacked the floor as hard as he could! The x-ray showed that it was not broken. However, we had church that night and everyone wanted to shake his hand. With every handshake, he repented. We laughed about it later, and we needed to lighten up anyway! We were both wrong and we both suffered consequences.

Go Ahead and Laugh!

I am reminded of the day, many years later: we were sitting on the sofa and David said, "Look! A spider!" I looked down at my leg and sure enough there was a Grand-Daddy Long Legs on me. I screamed and smacked it off as he was laughing hysterically.

Then I said, "Oh no, it's on you now!" Then he screamed and smacked it off of his leg while I laughed hysterically. Poor spider was probably dead by that time. The truth is that we all need to be able to laugh at ourselves and with each other and not get so easily offended. The Psalmist said, "Great peace have they which love thy law and nothing shall offend them" (Psalm 119:165 KJV). When you are secure in the promises of God, the truth about yourself and how God feels about you, life can be a lot more peaceful. Things people say and do just do not affect you the same. We, however, were not there yet!

The Odd Couple

On top of our anger and offense, we had very little in common. One of David's means of unwinding was to ride his motorcycle. I rode with him a few times, but, for me, it was like riding a horse. I made myself ride horses again after I left home, so I could get over the fear of the accident, but I never enjoyed it. Likewise, I had also been thrown from a motorcycle in an accident with my first husband, and he could actually see! While I rode with David a few times, it was difficult for me to enjoy it, and I finally stopped.

David loved to go to the gym. I sat on the bleachers from the time of my brain surgery in fourth grade until I graduated high school because no one had any idea what would happen to me if I was overexerted. I was a physical enigma to the medical community and probably, to the school, a liability. Naturally, I learned to hate the gym.

David loved to get up early. Feeling ambivalent about the job and the arguments we had so often stopped our morning bike rides. I was more naturally a night owl anyway and gravitated back to staying up late. The only reason I got up early was to dress and get to work on time.

Finding common ground

Today, as couples in counseling experience a lack of common recreation, I ask them to create a list of three to five things that neither of them do but are open to trying together, and then make that time together as enjoyable as possible. Why? It is because couples who spend time together in times of greatest enjoyment find it easier to stay together.

I also encourage couples to befriend other healthy couples so that the women can talk to the women and the men can encourage the men in more natural conversation. Communicating with the opposite sex is challenging because men and women listen through their deepest needs, and their deepest needs are nothing alike! Communication between a man and woman takes a selfless attitude to master.

Married couples need to make each other the number one priority under their relationship with God. However, they also need to take a break from each other now and then to think and process about how to resolve a conflict, to think about their input on an important decision, for personal reflection or devotions, or to do something that they may individually enjoy on occasion. In the long run this is healthy, and as long as they communicate their needs and remain "otherly-minded," they will not go overboard in any one area.

Not wrong, just different

David and I used to judge each other for being different. Someone always had to be right and someone had to be wrong. Our particular choices, however, did not make us wrong, just different. In fact, Dr. Walt & Barbara Larimore talk about this difference in their book, "His Brain, Her Brain". They write, "The two areas of the limbic system are far larger and more active in women than in men to the verbal and emotion handling centers of the brain. Therefore, women connect to words, feelings, and memories much more powerfully than men."[1] Elsewhere they say, "When girls and women are under stress, they'll often look to each other for support and comfort. Not Males. When boys and men are under stress, they usually want to do something physical or be left alone" (as cited in Sax, Why Gender Matters, 83).[2] Because of the larger emotional center in women's brains, they are usually more intentional about resolving issues of the heart than men.

In a mature world, these differences create a great opportunity for teamwork. As men can study how their wives, without words, trust the Lord to resolve their internal struggles, they witness a good example to follow. Once that level of trust is built in a marriage, men can also begin to allow their wives to operate in their role. As "helpers," women can guide them and help them to connect better with their own emotional struggles, finding resolution sooner than later. A woman in this privileged position must honor her husband by not shaming him into this behavior with her words. In the same way, men must treat women as an equal in the sight of God but as the weaker, more vulnerable gender. They must understand that where they can compartmentalize their emotions very well, women are not as good at doing this. Therefore, men need to live with women in patient understanding as they work through their own, more complex emotions, especially during a season of physical changes such as puberty for daughters, and pregnancy, post-partum, and menopause for women. This is the wisdom of 1 Peter 3:1-8.

Strength and commitment

I look at us now and wonder what we would do without each other. As we have grown up together, we have worked through a host of trust issues and have helped each other adjust in the midst of challenges, such as David's diminishing eyesight. Both of us still have a strong will. We both still have strong opinions. We still debate the WHY of our choices. The difference is that today, in addition to a strong commitment to staying together, we honor the Lord by respecting each other more. We also finish our conversations and conflicts to resolution. We give each other more grace and the benefit of the doubt. We apologize and forgive where necessary, and we try to end the day well, no matter how difficult. Our temperaments (the "how" of behavior) are different. Our personalities (the "why" of behavior) are different. Thankfully, these parts of our make-up have been forged in the fire! Looking back twenty-seven years to those first years of marriage, I see just how much fire it took to get us to where we are today! Some days, even now, require more fire!

Many days, the strong belief that we are meant to be together is what literally held us together. Belief is a powerful thing. When we heard God in that season of fasting and prayer, we REALLY heard Him. That is the beauty of hearing God's voice. When you really hear Him, it changes something inside of you. It is truth so powerful that it never lets go of you, but it melts into your lifestyle, and you begin to change without thinking; you never let go of it either.

Moments of surrender

We finally got over punching walls, kicking desks, smacking floors, turning over tables, and such, but our communication was still immature. He ran away from me so many times that we called it "Jump on your pony and ride!" I thought I would never get him to finish a conversation, but I was ignorant, and I had yet to resolve my fear, insecurity, rejection, abandonment, and so on. I spoke to him out of my pain, and he could not hear it. I did not know that I needed to speak to him as I would to Jesus (Ephesians 5:22). I did not have the maturity to honor him when he did not know how to be sensitive to my needs.

David had no idea how to nourish and cherish me (Ephesians 5:28-29). I would ask the Lord to help me submit to David. Then later, in an argument, as we were standing toe to toe with voices raised, he would draw a line in front of me with his foot and say, "That's it sister, don't cross it!" I would clench my fists and scream! But I did not cross the line. It was certainly not the way to live with me in understanding, but it was the first glimpse of my desperate desire to get my heart right. I was more determined to break the raging pain within and surrender any way that I could than I was determined to win the argument when we first started fighting. I began to ask for God's help more and more. I had little idea how to get free, but I knew the principle of asking, seeking, and knocking. I thought I would knock until

I knocked the door down! The more I prayed, the more things came to the surface and it was always ugly and painful.

By this time in our marriage, I thought I was losing my mind a time or two. I know he thought I was crazy more than a time or two. I wanted him to help me, but when he tried, I would push him away. I did not trust him, or any other man for that matter. At times, my vain imaginations would run wild. God knew that David did not have the ability to fix me. Besides, he was treading the water of his own internal battles. That left him at a deficit of the patience and courage it took to weather the storms with me. Sometimes men and women come into marriage so heavy with their own struggles that they have little to nothing leftover to give each other. This is why we should unpack our past, emotional bags BEFORE we marry, and it is something I offer and strongly suggest in pre-marriage counseling.

People can be so stubborn, and sometimes it seems like they are banging their heads against a wall over and over and over again! My Coach was waiting for me to hit the wall—again. And this time, I would surrender another level.

I had been in the church all my life. Mama said I cut my teeth on a church pew. It was what I knew. But my entire spiritual walk could be described as someone standing outside the door of the Kingdom, talking into an intercom to Whomever was listening on the other side. I was finally ready to take a deep breath and step inside the gate. I had no idea what was behind that door. What I did know was that I was a mess. Marriage did not fix it. A new job did not fix it. Volunteering for more ministries did not fix it. I had to take a chance and trust the One who sat silently on the other side of that intercom (only because I did not know how to listen). Due to the lies in my head, as good as He had been to me, I think I was still afraid of what He might say.

Connecting the dots

One day my cry for help hit a crescendo and this time, a beautiful thing happened. It was as if the bowls in heaven got so full that they tipped over and poured out an answer

(Revelation 5:8). First, I felt a sudden peace. It was as if Someone had His arms around me. Then, I began to hear the voice of the Holy Spirit reminding me of how faithful the Lord had been to me in the past. In that moment, I was able to turn my eyes off of the pain and onto Him. He began to connect my current emotional pain with similar pain I had experienced in the past. As the present and the past connected, one by one, I began to have flashbacks of all the times I was scared or hurting. Then, with His supernatural help, my eyes were opened, and I remembered that in all of those times, I FELT SOMEONE THERE! He had been with me in the midst of my darkest storms. Then the dam began to burst. With a flood of tears, I became overwhelmed with gratitude.

Having these recollections, I realized that, for as much abandonment, suffering, calamity, and terror had plagued my life, God had been doubly good to me. Someone who prayed for me years later said that because of what I had been through, I had always seen the enemy as much bigger than God, but He saw my heart, and He was going to flip the coin and change my perspective. What a promise of healing! However, in order to receive that healing, I had to change my attitude. I had to stop looking at how much I had suffered and focus on how much He had suffered, and how much I had been spared. This entire experience caused me to realize how much I needed to know Him more so that I could trust Him more.

That was the beginning of my healing.

Determine the relationship

We can have a need-based acquaintance, a knowledge-based commitment, or we can have intimacy with the Lord. I define intimacy with God as having a biblical truth-based, experiential knowledge of God, combined with believing and resting in the fact that you are known by God. In my childhood, due to the long bouts of illness, the strange accident, and the terror of people who wished to hurt me, I would say that

God went out of His way to reveal Himself to me. But I was in darkness.

I had experienced Him but lacked knowledge about Him. My experiences needed the light of knowledge to go with them. It was tantamount to being saved by a masked Avenger, never knowing His true identity. I had seen miracles. I was a recipient of miracles, and I thank God that in my most formative years, I was raised in a culture of miracles. But, "Who was that masked Man?" I did not know enough about Him to trust Him or to yield myself to Him. He was always the friend I could talk to, but not one I trusted enough to hear.

Lacking the truth of God's word, I did not know how to resist or take authority over the enemy's constant attacks. I was still very much afraid of him. I had become fiercely independent to protect myself, and I was afraid to let God get too close. My condition reminds me of Nehemiah 9:17 which says, "They refused to listen and failed to remember the miracles you performed among them. They became stiff-necked and in their rebellion appointed a leader in order to return to their slavery. But you are a forgiving God, gracious and compassionate; slow to anger and abounding in love. Therefore you did not desert them." Likewise, He never gave up on me. He knew I would eventually surrender, and for that I am thankful!

I complained about why things did not go well. I kept asking for help. In spite of my immaturity, He graciously provided for me at certain times of need. Perhaps it was because I asked someone else to pray for me or with me. In any case, my inability to receive from Him cut off the blessings that could have been poured out on my life. I desperately needed His healing, and He was always available. The key was to yield and surrender something to Him and then receive something in return from Him. But I did not know how, so I remained busy ministering to others.

Triage Escapees

Have you experienced this yourself? Have you ministered to others for any length of time while feeling like you were walking through hell with your back broken? The Lord is good and faithful to express His love, power, and provision through our giftedness to meet the perceived needs of others. But what about our deepest needs? How many of us really know Him? How many really feel known by Him? For the many who can say yes to those questions, I meet many more who cannot. Having God's love, power, and provision moving through us to meet the perceived needs of others is better served for the purpose of evangelism—reaching the lost who do not know Him at any level. But all too often, we as Christians are more dependent on a person of flesh and blood than we are upon God to meet our own perceived needs, to give us direction, or to solidify our identity. There are some things we can do for each other, but I would imagine that, like marriage, we try to extract from one another things that only God can do for us.

He Was There all the Time

My experience was about to turn, albeit slowly, like turning the *Titanic*! I had a great deal to learn, and I still had some painful times on the way. But for now, I was in the moment with the Holy Spirit. Walking down memory lane with Him, I realized how I had almost died—several times—and how He was there to save me. Every time someone tried to hurt me, God either stopped or redeemed it. Every time the enemy tried to lure me away, God stepped between us. I could have been dead, injured or severely abused! I could have been lured away into the occult—several times—and yet God kept His hand on me. There was only so much my parents could do. So many times my circumstances were beyond their control. The Lord was already carrying out His plan for me even then by continuously taking what the enemy meant for my destruction and turning it around for my good (Romans 8:28). Yes, I still suffered greatly.

Through generational sin, there were doors open to the enemy before I could defend myself, but even more so in later years, as a result of my own sin and pride. This is how the enemy works. But it could have been much worse!

When I saw how much God had always been there and what He had done, I realized that He loved me. He loved ME, and I had a specific purpose or I would have already been dead! Like the Psalmist in Psalm 31:21, "...He showed me the wonders of his love when I was in a city under siege."

It reminds me of a song that goes, "He was there all the time. He was there all the time. Waiting patiently in line, God was there all the time." And He was. In fact, He was the only One that was there all the time. You may not be old enough to remember the Maytag Repairman. Maytag appliances boasted that they so rarely broke down that their poor repairman sat around the office all day waiting on a service call. I am certain that the Holy Spirit feels the same way. He has the answers to our problems. He has the answer to the direction we are to take. He has all the genius of the Godhead when we need a witty idea. Yet, in our independence, who really takes that much advantage of His availability? There are some who do, but there are far more Christians who live with a mere fire insurance policy rather than a title deed to their full inheritance.

I knew God could use me, but I had a SPECIFIC purpose to fulfill. In Ephesians 2:10, the scripture reads, "For we are his workmanship, created in Christ Jesus for good works, which God prepared beforehand, that we should walk in them." I had a long way to go yet, but God was showing me that I am a human BEING before I am a human DOING. I am more important than my purpose. And yet my purpose is important too! I had to learn more about them in that order. For me, that would take the next few years to learn.

Sometimes we are more works-oriented because we do not know or believe how much God loves us. We think we must earn our way into His heart so that He will hold our spot in eternity. Other times we are just not that comfortable with being still and receiving from anyone, especially God. So we remain busy. I was a bit of both. I knew He was there for me, but I had no idea all that His Word said about how much He loves me. I had also built high walls inside my heart to protect me. I had trouble receiving love from my husband as well as from the Lord.

Through this glorious experience, I opened my heart to a new level of relationship with the Kingdom Coach. I thanked Him for never leaving me alone and said, "Okay, Lord, I am ready."

Do You Know Him?

Speaking of opening your heart to the next level of relationship, I have to ask you a question. Have you ever opened your heart to Jesus as Savior and Lord? I understand that the majority of people who are more likely to read this book are also more likely to be Christians. However, I have met people who started going to church, got involved and even filled positions of leadership, but later realized that they had never actually surrendered their hearts and lives to Jesus as their Savior and Lord. They were trying to live a moral life but missing out on all of the great benefits of the Kingdom of God! Unless you're actually a "company man," you do not get the benefits! Like working a temporary position for a great company, but you feel somewhat like an outsider, you usually get less in return for your hard work, and you do not get the company benefits.

Of course, some people seek to be contract labor because they have issues with submitting to authority or they want to be in control. Not in every case, but sometimes. Maybe those are some of your internal struggles. Perhaps you might examine yourself to make sure that you are not already building a defense case against what I am about to offer.

If you are interested in starting a relationship with the most amazing Coach available, it is very simple. If you have already been experiencing a tug or a longing in your heart as you have been reading this book, the Holy Spirit is responding to the need of your heart, and He is drawing you into His presence. It is His desire to meet you right where you are at this moment. He is a "come as you are" God.

The great news is that you do not even have to change a thing about yourself before you come to Him because He has always loved you regardless of where you have been, what you have done, or what was done to you. There is nothing you can ever do that will make Him love you more, and yet there is nothing you can ever do that will make Him love you less!

"But what about all the bad things that have happened to me" you might say. You might think that bad things happen because God either does not exist or does not care. Neither is true. Like I illustrated in my own story thus far, because of sin in us or even around us, we become open game for a real enemy who hates us and seeks to destroy us. Without being in covenant with God, you do not have the benefit of authority over the devil. And if you think your life is going great without God, look carefully – you probably have people praying for you – standing in the gap for your salvation and for your good. The enemy will set you up with a line of "sin credit," but he always comes to collect the bill before long, and you always pay with interest. He is on a "seek and destroy" mission (John 10:10; 1 Peter 5:8), and he can masquerade as an angel of light–a bastion of goodwill (2 Corinthians 11:14). Yet he remains, "the father of lies" (John 8:44).

Here is the gospel simply put:

John 3:16 states, "For God so loved the world, that he gave his only Son, that whoever believes in him should not perish but have eternal life."

Romans 3:23 states, "For all have sinned and fall short of the glory of God." We were all born with the sinful, human nature passed down from Adam, and that sin made us fall short of God's standard – or the ability to safely dwell in the presence of a Holy God without immediate judgment.

Romans 6:23 states, "For the wages of sin is death, but the free gift of God is eternal life in Christ Jesus our Lord."

Carrying the weight of sin demands a punishment. But God has given His son so that we can trade our sin for eternal life through Jesus.

Romans 5:8 states, "But God shows his love for us in that while we were still sinners, Christ died for us." See, God loves us even BEFORE we come to Him.

Finally, Romans 10:13 tells us that everyone who calls on the name of the Lord shall be saved! Romans 10:9 tell us that "If you confess with your mouth, 'Jesus is Lord,' and believe in your heart that God raised Him from the dead, YOU WILL BE SAVED!" [Emphasis mine]. We must believe that HE IS: He is Lord, He is God's Son, He is the perfect Lamb that was slain for our sin, He is risen and seated with God right now praying for us!

If you find yourself at a loss for words, but feel a witness to this in your heart, please take a moment and pray the prayer below. Praying a canned prayer does not necessarily make you a believer unless you believe! However, it helps to put your new beliefs into words and as you hear those words coming out of your mouth, brings your heart and mind into agreement. I hope you are ready!

"Lord Jesus, I know now that I am a sinner. Not only was I born a sinner because of the fall of Adam, but I have sinned. I may not know much, but I believe that God loves me, and I want to learn more about that love. I believe that You are the Son of God and that You died in my place. I am forgiven because You took my punishment on the cross. Right now, I accept that forgiveness through the sacrifice that You made for me. I receive the salvation that You purchased with Your precious blood. I look forward to getting to know You, the Father, and the Holy Spirit through the Bible. Thank You for saving me. Thank You God for receiving me as Your child. I AM GRATEFUL! Amen."

If you prayed that prayer or something like it in your own words just now, angels are LITERALLY rejoicing over your decision (Luke 15:7). They are waiting to watch over you and minister to you in this life (Hebrews 1:14). You are about to learn how to be a disciple. You GET to develop a relationship with God and discover how much He loves you, how good He is, and that He wants to partner with you in this life before eternity. Congratulations, and welcome to the Kingdom! Keep reading because you will discover how to grow, probably faster than I did. Just read and learn from the chapters that follow and apply what you learn. You will make it! Pray for God to lead you to a church that focuses on discipleship so you can take this journey with others. Get involved where you can and get to know other Christians who can encourage you (Hebrews 10:25). No church is perfect, but there are some great Christians still out there in spite of what you hear about hypocrisy. Although true in some cases, it is more a negative belief to keep you from taking your position in of the body of Christ (1 Corinthians 12:12-26). For more encouragement about how the Father feels about you, go to youtube.com and search for "The Father's Love Letter." Watch and enjoy!

Search Me, O God

Others of you may know about the Coach, and you know that He lives inside of you. If, however, you realize that you do not acknowledge Him as much as you could, then I have great news! You can start now!

He is faithful beyond all comparison. That is His reputation. At salvation, once the Spirit is in you (John 14:16-17), He has promised not to leave you (Hebrews 13:5-6). Isn't that beautiful? That is why the Word of God says, "...do not grieve the Holy Spirit of God" (Ephesians 4:30). We grieve Him because He is stuck with us by the Lord's own promise to never leave nor forsake us. If you look at the context of that entire passage, it is a laundry list of sins to put away and an exhortation to "... put off your old self" and to "walk in the newness of life" that you have been given through salvation. Why? The Holy Spirit, who is in you, is grieved. Everywhere you go, everything you say, everything you choose to watch on television, everything you read, everything you do in secret; the Holy Spirit has to endure it all, and it grieves Him. In fact, I would guess that His grief is the conviction that we feel inside. It is almost like a tightening in your gut. When we do or say something wrong, it is that instant "tug" at our hearts – His grief – that leads us to repentance.

Why do 1 John 1:9 and 1 John 2:1 tell Christians they still need to repent if they sin? First, you need to be sorry for grieving the One who never leaves you and has to be a party to your choices. He is part of the Godhead, and He is Holy. Second, you need to be accountable to God and to yourself for a continued renewing of your mind. Repentance is changing your mind completely about something, ridding yourself of all ties with it, forsaking it completely. It is changing what you believe about something. Your beliefs are the reigns of your behavior. You act upon what you feel, what you think, and what you believe. This is why King David said in Psalm 139:23-24,

> "Search me, O God, and know my heart! [Beliefs] Try me and know my thoughts! [Thinking] And see if there be any grievous way [Emotions] in me, and lead me in the way [Behavior] everlasting!"

No Gratitude is a Bad Attitude

A dear friend once said, "No gratitude is a bad attitude." On the other hand, gratitude is the greatest antidote for legalism. I realize that I had a measure of gratitude throughout my life. It is the reason I kept acknowledging God's presence, talking to him whenever I felt alone. I started out with a bit more spiritual discipline when David and I were first married, but the enemy used our issues and differences to steal it from me. The barrage of negative experiences also tried to steal that gratitude and prove that God was not good. But now I was armed with something very precious. If you serve God out of a continuous gratitude for Jesus and what He did for you on the cross, will you run to and not from God's presence? That is a thousand times better than feeling like you just cannot DO enough to stay in the Lamb's Book of Life! If I give you a list of rules and you try to keep them, you might do well for a while, but unless you are transformed from the inside by a strong belief, you will soon give up or be miserable trying to obey the rules in the strength of your flesh. I am so thankful that I finally saw the truth. The heaviness lifted after I learned the beauty of gratitude. You become like the object of your focus. Get your eyes on Jesus and what he did. Get them off of your sin, weakness, and failure. You will change and you will hardly even notice. Life began when I looked for Him, took His hand and started walking with Him. I wanted to get to know Him because He had been so good to me.

VIP Appointments

To close this chapter, I want to tell you that there are two VIP's in my life. The single most important appointment that must take precedence over everything else in my life is the open-ended appointment with the Kingdom Coach. I may have taken the hardest road and the longest distance to arrive, but I finally came to the place where He and I exchange conversation throughout the day, and sometimes the night. My life today reminds me of something Smith Wigglesworth said years ago, "I don't pray any longer than twenty minutes, but I never go twenty minutes without praying."

The other VIP in my life, with whom I have daily appointments for prayer, for feedback, for direction, and for intimate fellowship is my husband. I can finally say that he is a blessing to my life. Thankfully, he can finally say the same about me. We are not perfect by any means, but we are one, we are grateful, and after twenty-seven years and what it took to get us here, we do not want to hit the restart button on that process!

In John 16:33a Jesus said, "In this world you will have tribulation…" The enemy is hard after us, from the womb to the grave, to steal, kill, and destroy anything and everything he can in regards to our life, our faith, and our destiny. However, Jesus also said, "but take heart; I have overcome the world" (verse 33b). In this world, each of us will suffer to various degrees. But suffering, the Word of God says in many verses (1 Peter 2:19, 2 Timothy 2:3, Romans 5:3), has a way of perfecting our character in so many ways. So we have a choice. Life in this world can make us bitter or better. Suffering has a purpose and I thank God for the suffering that cultivated a heart to walk with my Coach. If I had not responded to Him as I did, I am not sure that I would be much farther down the road in character or maturity than I was years ago.

All Honor and Praise to Him!

> "When I think about the Lord—how He saved me, how He raised me; How He filled me with the Holy Ghost, how He cleansed me to the uttermost. And when I think about the Lord, how he picked me up and turned me around, how He placed my feet, on solid ground. It makes me want to shout, 'Hallelujah! Thank You Jesus! Lord You're worthy, of all the honor, and all the glory and all the praise—honor and praise."[3]

From Religion to Relationship

Chapter Four

Personal Application

1. On a scale of 1-10, how would you rate yourself on keeping a commitment? 1 2 3 4 5 6 7 8 9 10

2. What three parts are necessary in helping us keep our commitments?
_____ _____ _____

3. Concerning commitments, what is the better perspective to have: ☐ I GET to do this   ☐ I HAVE to do this

4. Have you ever used busyness to run away from the responsibility of a commitment?   Yes   No

5. What was the important question to ask in response to the sermon, *One More Night with the Frogs*?
_____

_____

6. Do you remember a time in your life when the stress was so oppressive that it surfaced your soul scum? What did you do and what did you learn?
_____

_____

_____

7. When is the best time to deal with your pain?
_____

8. Sometimes it is difficult to identify painful emotions or why they exist. Have you ever hidden hard to identify painful emotions behind the door of anger?   Yes   No

9. If you have dealt with sinful anger, can you see where it opened a door to the enemy in your life?   Yes   No

10. If you are married, what was your biggest take away from this chapter?

_____

_____

11. List at least three ways that couples can have greater strength and commitment in marriage?

_____

_____

12. Have you ever prayed for something until it seemed like the bowls of heaven poured out your answer? Yes No If so, What happened?

_____

13. Describe a time in your life when you heard God's voice so strongly that it transformed your thinking, your emotions, or your direction? Describe how you heard Him (the Word, in your heart, spoken in a vision, etc.).

_____

_____

14. Which describes your current relationship with God?
a) Knowledge-based acquaintance
b) Need-based commitment
c) Intimacy

15. Did you know that God is more concerned for YOU personally than what you do for the Kingdom? Sometimes we focus on being busy because we do not know that He cares that much or we are afraid to receive from Him. If you are more works-oriented, for which reason are you this way?
a) I did not realize He cared that much
b) I am not comfortable with receiving from Him

16. Would you say that you practice religion or have a relationship with God?

_____

_____

17. Do you believe that you have a specific purpose to fulfill in your lifetime?   Yes   No
Why or why not? _____

_____

18. Do you agree that the most important appointment you should keep is to meet regularly with the Kingdom Coach? If you did not answer "yes" but you consider obtaining counsel from the Kingdom Coach as something you would like to do, what is prohibiting you?

_____

_____

19. Provoke yourself to gratitude by asking the Lord to show you times He was there for you. Pray and write what you remember. Next, read the story of the crucifixion (John 17:20). As you think about this story, can you see the incredible price He was willing to pay to free you from the slavery of sin? Write about what the cross means to you.

_____

_____

20. In light of this chapter, what are some "next right steps" that you would like to take?

_____

_____

_____

In closing

Father, in the Name of Jesus, we thank You for all that You planned from the beginning to bring us into a deep, meaningful, empowering relationship with You. I pray for our eyes of understanding to be enlightened to all that You have done. Lead us through Your Word to find this truth so that our hearts may be overwhelmed with gratitude. We understand from Your Word in Ephesians that our works are important; they are designed specifically for each of us to play a role in expanding the Kingdom of God. Before we would even seek You for confirmation about those things, enlarge our understanding of how much more you care about US than what we will ever do. Then we will have the confidence we need to complete any task You have specifically designed for us. Thank You for not leaving us to ourselves. You have given us all we will ever need for life and godliness. For THAT truth alone, we can be grateful. Open our eyes to the great Father you became for us. Help us to embrace the power of the cross and resurrection every day. Sharpen our focus to remain upon You. We love You, Abba. Amen.

Chapter Five

FREEDOM FROM BIBLICAL ILLITERACY

"For the word of God is living and active, sharper than any two-edged sword, piercing to the division of soul and of spirit, of joints and of marrow, and discerning the thoughts and intentions of the heart" (Hebrews 4:12).

As a counselor, when I assess the needs of my clients, one of the common answers I hear is that they have problems progressing past a certain stage in their spiritual lives and/or they might even say that their life problems have become worse since they became a Christian. At that time, one of the questions I usually ask them in response is "Have you read your Bible?" If they have not read it all the way through and they are not prone to the daily reading or devotional reading, then it is the first prescription I give them. It is the easiest way to resolve those problems. You cannot apply what you do not know.

What if some people are having problems and they HAVE read through their Bible and even read it devotionally? That is when I know that there are usually deeper negative beliefs contained within them, ones that have never been identified. These beliefs continuously attack their identity. This was the problem I struggled with for several more years.

Monkey See, Monkey Do!

After I had the breakthrough encounter with the Coach, my life began to calm down in regard to the relationship with my husband and with others as well. It tempered my personality, which is what I needed. It was easier to be myself. I did not feel nearly as defensive, and I was more able to stop sweating the small stuff.

After watching David keep up with his daily spiritual disciplines I began reading my Bible a bit more. I was already accustomed to talking to the Lord, but following this new level of surrender, I changed my prayer time to include a few minutes of waiting at the end, just to see if I could hear Him consistently. For a while, I remember that I would actually get down on the floor face down and shield my eyes and squint, as if that would help me hear better. I did hear on some occasions, but I eventually learned that I did not have to "assume the position."

One day, while I was waiting, I felt an urgency to read the Word in a different way. As the Coach's new apprentice, He impressed on my heart to read more than the book of John, more than the New Testament; He wanted me to read the entire Bible! At that moment, I remembered that David was reading a *One-Year Bible*. It was a gift his brother had given him for Christmas. It had three hundred sixty-five, once-a-day readings broken down into passages from the Old Testament, New Testament, Psalms and Proverbs. It looked interesting, so I went to the bookstore and found a copy of my own. At the bookstore, holding a *One-Year Bible* in my hand, I thought, "Hmm. Will I have the patience to make it through Lord?" It would become an incredible new journey for me.

Father Wounds

Father wounds are what many counselors refer to in regard to how we have been wounded by our natural fathers, and those wounds are extremely valid. However, I like to refer to Father wounds as anything that keep us distant from the love of the Father, which would include the wounds from our natural fathers, our mothers, misconceptions about God, lies we are told about Him, and so on.

I was quite comfortable with the Holy Spirit and, although there was much more to learn about Jesus, because of what I knew about the cross, I was comfortable with Him. The story of the crucifixion and a simple presentation of the gospel was something our church did very well when I was a child, and I loved Jesus. However, I was still a bit unsure about God as a Father. Because I was just beginning to read my Bible, I had no true concept of Him other than the impressions I was given growing up in church. For me, those first impressions were not positive.

First impressions of Father God

As a child, I had always been under the impression from other Christians and preachers that He was angry at us all. Mom was involved in ministry from my early youth. She taught Sunday school and led the children's choir. I remember her teaching us Bible verses, but none of them ever stuck like the only two I remembered (Hebrews 11:1, John 3:16). I even took catechism in my younger teens. I remember, "What is the Bible?" "The Bible is The Book—the Word of God." "Who wrote the Bible?" "Holy men of God wrote the Bible," and so on. I know that it helped strengthen my foundation, but my problems demanded a much larger sword!

In my formative years, I also heard many sermons about hell. The church showed movies about hell. I knew for sure that there was a heaven to gain, BUT THERE WAS SURELY A HELL TO SHUN! The message of eternal judgment is fine because it is the truth. The Bible says so. Not only is God loving (1 John 4:8-10), gracious (Exodus 33:19; 1 Pet. 2:3), and merciful (Exodus 34:6; Psalm 67:1; James 5:11), He is also holy (Isaiah 6:3; Rev. 4:8), just (Neh. 9:32-33; 2 Thess. 1:6), and hates sin (Psalm 5:5-6; Hab. 1:13). God punishes the sinner (Jer. 50:31; Ezekiel 44:12; Matt. 25:46; 2 Thess. 1:9; 2

Pet. 2:9; Heb. 10:29). People have reportedly died and gone to hell. Then they come back to tell about it. People I know have watched others who do not know Christ at the point of death, drawing their last breath with a ghastly, terrorized look on their faces as they went. I have not visited hell myself, but I have encountered quite a few demons that belong there, and I am very thankful there is a final destination waiting for them! But hell was not created for man (Matthew 25:41). Preaching a message about eternal judgment is fine because people need to be warned. However, the message when I was a child was always fear based, even though it always ended with John 3:16.

The message of eternal judgment needs to be balanced with the love of God. In fact, I would say that it needs to be the primary message. People need to know WHY it is important that they do not want to go to hell. It is not primarily because "the worm dieth not and the fire is not quenched" although that is true (Mark 9:44 KJV). It is not primarily because "there will be weeping and wailing and gnashing of teeth" although that is also true (Matthew 13:50). For goodness sake, tell them WHY it is important that they do not want to go there! It is because they will be eternally separated from the Father (2 Thessalonians 1:9). Is that not a better motivation to keep people out of hell–to teach them how much the Father loves them? "…see what great love the Father has lavished on us, that we should be called children of God" (1 John 3:1). If you have received salvation through Jesus Christ, you are a child of God! Once you have experienced His love, and once you realize that you will be eternally separated from His presence, that is a much better motivation for staying as far from hell as possible (as I was soon to discover).

Who's Your Daddy?

In John 14:9, Jesus said, "Anyone who has seen Me has seen the Father." God gave us a peak into His own nature, not only through the Old Testament, but through the person of Jesus. Those who focus on God's righteous wrath and the Divine Holiness of the Old Testament (as if that were the sum total of Who He is) should balance their perspective with the beautiful love of Jesus. We have incredible examples of the love of Jesus such as His interacting with the children (Mark 10:14, Luke 18:16). Another good one is Jesus weeping at the tomb of Lazarus (John 11:35), or when He wept over Jerusalem (Luke 19:41). How about when he LOVED the rich, young ruler (Mark 10:21), knowing he was going to walk away (Matthew 9:4) from his invitation to join the disciples? These are amazing glimpses of the heart of God the Father. In John 14:26, Jesus states that the Holy Spirit will teach us all things and remind us of everything that Jesus has already said.

Read Your Bible—All of It

As I pondered what to write about the Bible, I thought to include some of my favorite findings. I also included things that, in my experience, can save you some pain as you pursue healing, maturity, and your destiny. The greatest thing about the Bible is that once you put Scripture inside of you, the Holy Spirit will draw it out for you when you need it! God's Word is a powerful weapon of spiritual warfare and something I was missing for many years, simply through a lack of spiritual discipline.

The Power Team

I found a good bit of information about the Godhead: The Father, Son, and of course, the Holy Spirit, my Coach. God is on the throne of heaven (Isaiah 14:13, Matthew 5:34,23:22, Revelation 7:15). Jesus is seated in heavenly places, on a throne, at the right hand of God (Ephesians 1:20, Hebrews 12:2). Once He ascended to the throne beside His Father, which was the reward for giving His life, He could not be in two places at once, as He would forever have a glorified human body (Luke 24:39). But He did not want to leave man alone.

He wanted unbroken fellowship and communication with us (John 10:27, 16:12-15). He told the disciples it was better for Him to go away, but that when He ascended, He would ask the Father to send the Holy Spirit, Who would be with them and in them (John 14:16-17; Romans 8:9) as well as everyone who received salvation (Romans 8:9). We become a temple for the Holy Spirit to dwell (1 Corinthians 6:19). Inside each of us who are saved, we host the spiritual representative of Christ and of the Father, whereby God fulfilled his promise to never leave us nor forsake us (Hebrews 13:5). I love this!

There is unity among the Godhead. They work in our lives as a team! Before salvation, The Father was empowering the words of the gospel by the Holy Spirit to draw me to Jesus. At age six, when I received salvation, I not only knew about sin through the sermons I heard, I had already experienced sin's effects: through abuse, abandonment, sickness, and loneliness. I had enough experience and the cognitive ability to understand that I did not want to spend my life apart from Jesus. My fear actually drove me to Him. By the Spirit, even at that tender age, I knew I would somehow be safer with Him.

Divine benefits package

> His divine power has granted to us all things that pertain to life and godliness, through the knowledge of him who called us to his own glory and excellence. (2 Peter 1:3).

On that same day, when I received salvation, I was given a full benefits package, one I would not understand for a very long time. That day, the Holy Spirit came to live inside of my human spirit. He set up housekeeping and turned a light on. He would initiate a relationship with me, become my guide, and connect me to the Father through the Son, something I tangibly felt for only a few moments on my daddy's lap the day I was born again.

I have found so many people who do not know and/or believe their identity in Christ, and who do not know what is at their disposal from heaven's resources. It seems that the heavenly storehouse is full of accessible provisions which sit wrapped, like unopened Christmas packages with our names on them. They are still waiting for believers to requisition them through prayer.

My parents and I were in a similar situation. I think they would agree with me when I state that we lived more by the teachings and sermons of the church than we did by our own devotional knowledge of God through the Bible. That is not to say that the church did not teach the Bible, but there was so much we did not know, particularly about my situation. Life was busy, and the enemy did not want our family to make a discovery about the keys to our breakthrough. If the enemy cannot keep you idle and into trouble, he will keep you busy. Some never slow down enough to deal with what is going on inside. It is too painful. Many, like me, say that they pray all the time, but it seems that God does not hear them and does not answer. Many say that they feel that God does not love them, and they have struggled for years with a low sense of worth. Some have even considered giving up their faith. They do not know, and the enemy does not want them to know, that part of prayer should include the use of the authority Jesus gave us over the devil. After all, we are the peace-keeping forces in the earth, left to enforce the victory of Christ, and to carry on His work and in greater measure (John 14:12), to rescue souls from darkness, and shut down the enemy's operation of using people to do his work. (1 John 3:8, 2 Timothy 2:20-26).

Power of a positive memory

I had an experience in the mid-90's, one among many that changed my life. By this time, I had read the Word of God many times, but the Word was just beginning to read me. One night, while in prayer, I had a vision. I was standing in heaven with my back to the throne of God. I was staring at a large map. It was not a map of the world, rather a map of my life. God's hand came towards the map from over my head and

He pointed to a position where I was at that time in my life. I had already made a lot of progress building a good foundation and I had received quite a bit of training by that time. But He spoke to me and said in the most kind, but authoritative voice, "Here is where you are today." His finger began to slide all the way across the map until it landed on a spot signifying a place far from where He began, and He said, "And this is where you are supposed to be."

I remember how my heart broke. God was not condemning, not in the least. I believe the purpose for the vision was not to bring me to disappointment, as there was not a trace of disappointment in God's voice. In fact, His tone and demeanor was rather suggesting, "Take courage! I am going to help you." I believe God was giving me something upon which to focus: that I was in His presence and that He was going to help me reach the intended destination. That experience has helped me push forward in challenging or questionable circumstances ever since.

I recall a time in scripture when God made the same kind of memory for Jesus. I find great comfort, even confirmation, in Mark 9 and Matthew 17. The time was steadily nearing when Jesus would have to face the cross. In this passage, Jesus, took Peter, James, and John up a high mountain where He was transfigured before them. His clothes were dazzling white, and he was transfigured as if He had His glorified body. Moses and Elijah appeared and were talking to Jesus and Peter, James, and John saw them. What a scene and what a gift from the Father! Can you imagine? On the way to take on the unimaginable punishment that He did not deserve, the Father gives His Son a memory on that mountain that will carry Him all the way THROUGH the experience of the cross!

Romans 12:2 states that Jesus, "…for the joy set before Him endured the cross, despising the shame…" What was the joy set before Him? Perhaps it was on that mountain, where for a few moments, He felt the joy of a throne and a glorified body that awaited Him after He would make it all the way through the cross, death, burial, and resurrection. He felt what it was like to be in a glorified body. Maybe He saw the mercy seat where He would put His own blood to pay for the sins of man. No doubt, He was encouraged as the law (Moses) and the prophets (Elijah) confirmed His deity to His followers and the goal of His suffering to Him (Romans 3:21). Having that experience to look back on would help to carry Him through every moment of hardship from that point forward. Likewise, the power of a positive memory can help carry us through difficult circumstances. Jesus kept His eyes on the prize and He made it all the way. He did it for you and me and all those who call upon His name for salvation.

Now that Christ is seated on a throne beside the Father, He is praying for us (Hebrews 7:25). For those of us who are in Christ, the Kingdom Coach lives within to keep us connected to the loving heart of the Father and focused on the life of the Son!

Angels are watching over us

When I started my *One-Year Bible* journey, I still had an identity crisis. I had yet to fully understand who I was in Christ. Knowing what I know now about spiritual warfare, I am certain that, as I read, there was quite a skirmish going on around me. Like the parable of the sower, the enemy wanted to snatch the truth away, to scorch it with reminders of trouble and persecution, to choke it with anxiety and fear, and to make sure that I would question it with a spirit of offense: "If He could do all that, and He loves you, why did He not spare you?!" I can also imagine that there were angels bending near to whisper reminders of God's goodness. It seemed they were continuously fighting around me, and some days, it felt like I was caught in the middle!

I am thankful that as real as the demonic realm manifested itself, there was an equal share of angelic activity working on my behalf. The writer of Hebrews states concerning angels, "Are they not all ministering spirits sent out to serve for the sake of those who are to inherit salvation?" (Hebrews 1:14).

Although we do not worship these beings (Colossians 2:18), they get far less credence than the demonic realm. On the subject of angels, *Matthew Henry's Concise Commentary* states,

> "The angels minister to them [heirs of salvation] in opposing the malice and power of evil spirits, in protecting and keeping their bodies, instructing and comforting their souls, under Christ and the Holy Ghost."[1]

Also, concerning these angelic ministers who serve the body of Christ, *Gills Exposition of the Entire Bible* states,

> "the ministry of angels to, and for them, lies in things temporal and spiritual, or what concern both their bodies and their souls; in things temporal, in which they have often been assisting, as in providing food for their bodies, in curing their diseases, in directing and preserving them in journeys, in saving and delivering them from outward calamities, in restraining things hurtful from hurting them, and in destroying their enemies; in things spiritual, as in making known the mind and will of God to them, in comforting them, and suggesting good things to them, and in helping and assisting them against Satan's temptations; and they are present with their departing souls at death, and carry them to heaven, and will gather the elect together at the last day. And they are 'sent forth' to minister to them in such a way; they are sent forth by Christ, the Lord and Creator of them, who therefore must be superior to them; they do not take this office upon themselves, though, being put into they faithfully and diligently execute it, according to the will of Christ: and this shows the care of Christ over his people, and his kindness to them, and the great honour he puts upon them, to appoint such to minister to them; and since they are of so much use and service, they ought to be respected and esteemed, though not worshipped."[2]

Then I fell down at his feet to worship him, but he said to me, "You must not do that! I am a fellow servant with you and your brothers who hold to the testimony of Jesus (Revelation 19:10).

That reminds me of a conversation with a little girl at our church when she was only four. She said, "Look G'Ma! There are angels up there" as she pointed above the pastor's head. The grandmother asked, "What do they look like?" The little girl answered, "They are nice angels, not like the ones who fight outside with swords." Children who are raised in the truth develop a child-like faith that Jesus said we must have as adults if we are going to experience the Kingdom. If we do not have this faith, we miss so much. Jesus specifically said in Matthew 11:25, "I praise you, Father, Lord of heaven and earth, because you have hidden these things from the wise and learned, and revealed them to little children [or to the childlike]."

Are Angelic Encounters Legitimate?

I will give you two examples of angelic encounters I had in 2002. But first, I want to demystify the purpose for which I am about to share. Some people in the body of Christ are afraid to acknowledge the activity of angels among us. I believe that this is a perfect example of taking scripture out of context. Before you read my stories, please take a moment and read Colossians 2:8-23. In context, you will see that Paul is not teaching that to have visions and acknowledging the activity of angels in our world is to be prideful, having vain imaginations, or be puffed up! You can easily deduce that point if you read verse eighteen alone. If this were true, he would have to deny his own testimony as well as many others in the Old and New Testaments alike! Therefore, let us be on the same page about the purpose of his teaching. False teachers, such as New Age teachers or philosophers, will put angels in the place of Christ, making null and void His sacrifice as well as His mediation and intercession for us to God. Such teachers will not acknowledge His Lordship and will draw others to themselves by their detailed visions that do not necessarily originate from the work of the Holy Spirit. False signs and lying wonders (2 Thessalonians 2:9) take the place of the Divine interactions between God and man.

Angelic Encounter

One day, after I had been an intercessor for several years, the Coach instructed me to call a resident here in town and to say, "I am interested in the house you have for sale." That is all He told me to say. So I found the number, and when the lady of the house answered, I asked her the question just as I had been instructed. She said, "How did you know the house was for sale? We have not listed it yet."

I had no idea what God was up to, but He had certainly peaked my interest and she had made me a little nervous with her answer. So I said, "I really did not know it was for sale either, but the Lord obviously knew and said to call you."

She said, "Can you come over?"

I said, "I will be there soon."

I had never met this woman before, nor been to her home. As it turned out, this particular piece of property was going on the market but the sale was going to be opposed by a certain influential group in town. It was on the National Registry. The house was the hospital during the Battle of Stones River in the Civil War. The location of the property was considered a demilitarized zone that served both sides of the war. Of the major battles of the civil war, the Battle of Stones River had more casualties on both sides than any other battle. There were blood stains that remained in the original flooring of the house. I would come to find that it was an interesting place, brimming with spiritual activity.

When I arrived, I introduced myself and told the owners that I was the director of the local House of Prayer and on the way over, the Lord said that He wanted me to walk the entire perimeter of the property every day and seven times on the seventh day and to pray as directed each day. I had no idea why, I just knew that I heard Him, and she was confirming everything, so I figured that I was not crazy. (When you have been spared from death as many times as I had been by then, you do not have the heart or the courage to tell the Lord, "No," although it took me years of practice to obey instantly. More about that in book two.)

So I went every day for seven days, taking a different intercessor with me each day. There was no telling what was going to happen, and I did not want to be the only one to experience the adventure! Each day, the Lord instructed us what to ask Him in prayer. That is exactly what we did.

While we were prayer-walking the property, we saw visions of buildings placed in various locations and an African-American woman kneeling in the dirt, weeping and praying. Several intercessors reported seeing her in visions. As we inquired about the history of the property and the residents, each building we saw was exactly as it was on the original plantation. The woman was a slave that the landowner loved. She was a God-fearing woman, and when the war was over, she was given fifty dollars, a cow, and her freedom. This was all recorded in the history of the plantation. Interestingly, freedom was one of the things the Lord had us asking for on behalf of the city as we walked. But that is not even the best part!

I think it was around day five when one of my closest friends and prayer partners and I were standing in the spot where everyone kept seeing the woman. As we stood there, we looked all around the property to see if we could spot anything significant from her point of view. I assumed if I could see her, maybe I could see something else! Guess what? Standing just across a little ravine, probably six feet on the neighbor's property, we saw an angel standing by the tree. Not only did we see it, but we took a digital photo of it and it showed up on the photo! As I inquired of the Lord about the angel, the Lord gave me an impression that this angel encouraged the woman that one day, her feet would leave that property and she would be free and according to historical record, this indeed happened! (My arms are covered with goose bumps as I am typing).

On the sixth day, it was raining, and I wanted to wait until the rain stopped before I went to walk. I did not ask anyone to go with me because I knew I may end up walking in the rain if it did not stop. In fact, it did not stop until dusk. I called the owner and asked if I could come after dark. She told me that she and her husband were going out of town for the evening and that I was welcome to drop by anytime. I was still somewhat afraid of the dark at that time. But I wanted to keep my promise to the Lord. So I went. There were a few light-posts around the house, but about ten acres were completely dark and the ground was not really level. There were also a good many holes for various animals living in the ground.

I put on my boots and headed over to the property. I parked and got out of the car and walked onto the twelve acre property. I already felt creepy. So I stood at the barn and prayed, "Lord, I pray that the angels You have commissioned to accompany me on this prayer journey would keep me safe, keep my feet from stumbling in the dark, keep every demonic scheme from prospering and give me the assurance that they are here with me, in Jesus' Name." Then I began to walk.

I felt a peace wash over me, and I began to walk and pray as I felt directed. I walked in pitch dark all the way around the property and came back around the house and to the front where there was a gazebo. I sat on the gazebo to give God thanks and talk to Him for a while. It was the most precious night. The skies had cleared and the stars were bright. There was a cool breeze blowing. I was so peaceful I could have lain down and went to sleep.

When I got up to leave, I walked down the gravel drive to the car, which was lit by the lamp poles. Seeing my shadow was nothing new to me. But as I walked and sang I slowly stopped singing as I saw my shadow and then a towering shadow following just behind and beside me. I must confess, out of all the demonic experiences I have had, it is no comparison to what I feel in the presence of an angel. The only thing stronger or more sobering to me is to be in the glorious manifest presence of God. I stopped. It stopped. I started walking and it hesitated for a moment and then began following me again. That was my confirmation. I wanted to know for sure that I was not seeing double! So I began to talk to him. Of course, there was no answer, but he accompanied me all the way to my car. What an escort and what a night! Thank God we are not alone. We have the Holy Spirit living inside of us, and we have angels all around, fighting and ministering on our behalf. It is part of that benefits package!

You may be curious as to why the Lord had me go to the property to pray. I know I was. I prayed for the seven days and it was over. I left and never saw that couple again. They sold the property to the city. The house and all the buildings were torn down and a new road was laid right through the middle of the property as a new exit to the area was created from Interstate Twenty-four. Years passed and I kept questioning the Lord as to what the whole prayer adventure was about? Finally, the exit and new road were completed. So much new construction came into the area. Today it is a booming part of the city leading to the interstate, and every time I travel that new road, I think of that experience.

One day in late 2005, I was visiting with a friend who lives near the interstate. He said, "Did you see the newspaper this week?" I told him that I had not.

He said, "Did you hear that Exit 76 is now being called the portal to the gateway of the city?"

When he said those words to me, the Lord spoke to my heart and said, "That headline is the answer to your question about the prayer adventure. Do you remember what I asked you to declare each day on the property?"

As I thought about the ministries we asked and declared to be brought into existence, I realized that God had called various people in town to raise up each of these ministries – every single one.

The Lord said, "Important decisions, court cases, and public proclamations were always made at the city gate" (Genesis 23:18, 34:24, 2 Chronicles 32:6, Job 29:7-13). I know my jaw dropped. I just shook my head and smiled. There have also been a few times in the past five years, when a storm was approaching with severe tornado activity, the Lord told me to get in the car and drive out to Exit 76 and prophesy over the city in regard to our safety. I never had to question Him as to why.

Spiritual warfare is a personal responsibility

God's Word is a powerful weapon of spiritual warfare! In 1 Timothy 2:20-26, believers, in the household of faith, are compared to vessels of silver and gold or wood, hay, and stubble. The former are walking in freedom and set apart for a higher purpose. The latter are bound up in besetting sin, unhealed wounds, unforgiveness, and so on (v. 20-21). Paul is teaching Timothy how to deal with these "opponents" [those who oppose themselves v. 25, KJV] so that they may "cleanse themselves" (v. 21) from their condition through repentance. Why must they cleanse themselves through repentance? It is because Jesus already did His part. The power is available to surrender these things up for His healing, for deliverance, etc. What happens if they do not do this? If they do not, they remain enslaved by the devil, who has taken them captive to do his will (v. 26). This describes believers who have yet to get their eyes off of their sin, their mistakes, how they appear to others, and so on. "But you have no idea how I struggle over my pain and my sin" you might say. Remember, you become more of and more like the object of your focus. Surrender the object of your focus to Jesus, and then turn from it once and for all.

If you are stuck in a cycle of sin, such as addiction, one way to break free after repentance is to picture that sin nailed to the cross with Christ. If you are constantly reminded of how badly you think about yourself because of something that was done to you in the past, identify that false belief and ask the Lord for the truth. Once you know the truth, it will set you free! (John 8:32) Whatever you do, refuse to carry these things one step farther. (I am providing a tool to help you do this in chapter six.) You must make a decision to lay them down before the Lord. If you belong to Christ, there is a conviction within you that compels you higher. It is the grief of the Holy Spirit within you (Ephesians 4:30). Come to Jesus and find rest from whatever it is that makes you oppose yourself. Get out of the devil's snare. You are not his slave! Stop living like one! You have been redeemed with precious blood that was the currency that purchased your freedom – from everything that hinders. Come to the only One who can reveal the truth about your condition, and then never take your eyes off of Him again. There is nothing left to consider outside of Him. The old you died with Him! Stop acting like it is not true. That is why you are called a BELIEVER! Whatever issue has become the snare through which the enemy is holding onto you, repent for carrying it one moment longer! Refusing to call on Him in repentance, for more grace (James 4:6) and mercy is our sin. "So whoever knows the right thing to do and fails to do it, for him it is sin" (James 4:17). Finally, renounce agreement with the devil, which has been holding you and controlling you, keeping you from that higher purpose to which you have been called.

Let's go back to the illustration I shared in Chapter Two about walking close behind the Holy Spirit. Colossians 3:1-10 says,

> "Since, then, you have been raised with Christ, set your hearts on things above, where Christ is, seated at the right hand of God. Set your minds on things above, not on earthly things. For you died, and your life is now hidden with Christ in God. When Christ, who is your life, appears, then you also will appear with him in glory.

As we continue walking closely behind or "in step" with the Spirit (Galatians 5:25), we remain "hidden" with Christ in God. As God sees us, now looking at us through the blood of His Son, we have been crucified with Christ (Galatians 2:20), we have been buried and raised with Him (Colossians 2:12), and we are seated in positional authority with Him in heavenly places (Ephesians 2:6) far above all the power of the enemy. However, the caveat here is to remain in that position through obedience, coming from a heart of gratitude (John 14:15). The question is whether or not, in our beliefs, our thinking, our emotions, and our behavior, we will remain "far above" the power of the enemy.

Let's keep reading verses 5-10:

> Put to death, therefore, whatever belongs to your earthly nature: sexual immorality, impurity, lust, evil desires and greed, which is idolatry. Because of these, the wrath of God is coming. You used to walk in these ways, in the life you once lived. But now you must also rid yourselves of all such things as these: anger, rage, malice, slander, and filthy language from your lips. Do not lie to each other, since you have taken off your old self with its practices and have put on the new self, which is being renewed in knowledge in the image of its Creator.

How do you remain above your enemy? You walk in the Spirit, allowing the Coach to give you the divine power necessary to deny your flesh and walk in obedience. See, you are never expected to do it alone. As you do it with His help, the resulting obedience not only brings the blessings of God down, it also protects you from the hand of the enemy and keeps you in a place of authority.

We need to not only remain safely in step with our Coach, we also need to know the Word! I believe that ignorance played the biggest part in the spiritual warfare that engulfed my life. We did not understand at the time that children can not only learn the Word but also understand basic concepts of spiritual warfare—and I would add that they need it! There is no Junior Holy Spirit! From the time we are saved, we have access to Him, regardless of whether we are four or forty! I am reminded of a time when a grandparent came to me for help. She said that her grand-daughter had been talking to an imaginary friend for a couple years. However, her imaginary friends were now showing up at night after she slept, and they were not nice any longer. In fact they were scaring her and tormenting her. She did tell her parents but they did not believe her. And of course, the visitations did not stop either. So the grandmother came and asked me what she should do. I told her to have a little Bible study with her granddaughter about her authority in Christ. Then I told her to instruct her granddaughter to first acknowledge God (James 4:7a) by saying, "Thank You Lord for being here with me tonight" and then when her little friends showed up to sit up in bed and tell them, "You are not my friends! I know who you are and I do not want you here anymore! In the Name of Jesus, I command you to leave and don't come back!" (James 4:7b). I said that if they, by chance, resisted her, to stand her ground and continue saying, "In the Name of Jesus, leave! And don't come back!" The little girl did this and it stopped. Children, who believe in their authority in Christ, by faith, have the full support of the hosts of heaven, who then go forth and war on their behalf. Children have such great faith and when they exercise their faith, it works! I taught my daughter the same principles and one day when I was under attack and desperately needed prayer, without hesitation, she laid hands on me and began to take authority over the devil in boldness. Not only did the enemy let go, but healing came soon thereafter!

> He called a little child to him, and placed the child among them...See that you do not despise one of these little ones. For I tell you that their angels in heaven always see the face of my Father in heaven (Matthew 18:2, 10-11).

The Whole Counsel of God

Reading the entire Bible brings greater understanding of the story of God and man, and particularly, as you read it in context. Isolating scriptures without knowing the context of the stories can be hazardous. You can easily take passages out of context and use them to mean something not intended by the writer or the Author. Reading the whole book in context also gives you a great picture of the heart of God. Knowing the heart of God makes me a woman after His heart! Look at the favor King David had for taking the posture of being a man after God's heart!

Doing the Word

The next year I read the whole Bible all over again, followed by another year. The year following that, I got over my fear of marring "The Book," cracked the binding and pulled out some markers. I decided to break it down for different purposes each year. One year I would highlight all of the promises.

As a result of his reading, David had recently written, *Doing the Word: Faith into Action for New Testament Christians.* He simply took all of the action verses and pulled them together into one manuscript. So that year, I also highlighted all of the verses commanding us to "do" something. Next, I highlighted all of the prayers. I was making the Bible one of the things it was intended to be: a consumable. Finally, I purchased a chronological *One-Year Bible*. That was cool because it put all the books in the order that they were actually written. The Scriptures really came alive to me that time!

Juiced up on the Word!

One weekend, I asked some friends if I could borrow their garage apartment and stay there for the weekend. They agreed. I took my Bible, a gallon of grape juice, and my boom box and tapes (Yes, cassettes). I worshipped and did nothing but read through the New Testament. It was better than Red-Bull!

The more I read the Bible, the more I want to read it. Today, David and I are like loaded guns—and not because we are angry, thank God! The amount of the Word that you put into your heart will come back to you as the Spirit of God draws it out and teaches you which parts to use (Luke 12:12) in teaching, in prayer, and in taking authority over the devil. He is the Spirit of truth and He is a great guide. Once you put the

Word in, He can send the right words back out and perfectly for every occasion!

He that hath ears to hear

I realized that when Jesus spoke to me or communicated anything from the Father, the Holy Spirit is actually the One who spoke. John 16:13-15 states,

> When the Spirit of truth comes, he will guide you into all the truth, for he will not speak on his own authority, but whatever he hears he will speak, and he will declare to you the things that are to come. He will glorify me, for he will take what is mine and declare it to you. All that the Father has is mine; therefore I said that he will take what is mine and declare it to you.

Once I got over my unbelief and fear about hearing God speak to me, I heard Him! I realized that as I read the Word, He would illuminate Scriptures to me and for me specifically according to my need. I also learned that when I asked Him a question, He would provide me an answer (Jeremiah 33:3, John 10:27). I worried for a while that the enemy was talking and I would not know the difference, but after reading the Bible and learning the character of God, I realized that John 10:5 was true! I was actually able to distinguish between the voice of the Holy Spirit and the voice of the enemy, and I could shut him down as soon as I recognized him!

Romans 10:17 states, "So faith comes from hearing, and hearing through the word of Christ." There are two Greek words for "word" in Scripture. Logos is the written word or the living Word of Christ (2 Timothy 2:15; John 1:1). Rhema is the spoken word of God, whether spoken out loud by you and me, spoken out loud through preaching, a scriptural illumination by the Holy Spirit, or the spoken Word of God into our spirit. Most scholars translate that scripture to mean that faith comes by hearing the Word of God spoken out loud, and we are able to hear it because the preaching of the Word was commissioned to men by God. That makes sense. However, I have also learned by experience that my faith is strengthened by hearing God's Word [His voice] speaking straight to my spirit when I inquire of Him or when I am teaching or counseling: "faith comes by hearing…"

In addition, my hearing [the ability to hear His voice] is sharpened as I continuously hear the spoken Word of God, whether I am reading it aloud, it is being read to me, or I am hearing God speak: "and hearing by the word of God." It is a continuous cycle. My ears become "sharp" the more I read the Scripture aloud and the more I quote it in teaching, preaching, and counseling. The Holy Spirit is talking all the time! Once you sit quietly for a moment and really listen, you literally have to break away and do something to stop hearing Him! I went from straining to hear the Lord at first to hearing Him all the time throughout the day. That took years, but it increased the more I read, memorized, quoted, heard, and spoke the Word of God.

Keep it simple

When I first began to read, true to my temperament, I wanted to keep things very simple. I rarely questioned what I read in the Bible. I was more like the blind man in John Chapter Nine. Jesus healed the man by putting mud on his eyes and then sending him to the pool of Siloam to wash it off. Once the man was healed, the Pharisees questioned him vehemently about who healed him? When he said, "It was Jesus," they stumbled over his answer because they believed Jesus was a sinner since He healed on the Sabbath. They questioned the man's family and then came back to question him again! They were outraged that Jesus did a miracle and it worked! The Pharisees became frustrated, and here is how the blind man silenced their high-minded inquisition: "…they called the man who had been blind and said to him, 'Give glory to God by telling the truth…we know this man is a sinner!' Then the blind man replied, 'Whether he is a sinner or not, I don't know! One thing I do know. **I was blind but now I see!**'" (John 9:24-25).

I read the Word and believed what it said. If the Word said it, I believed it. If the Word said I should not do something that I knew I was doing, I felt convicted and stopped. Conviction of the Holy Spirit is the key to "stopping" any kind of behavior that is contrary to the Word. As a word of caution, do not tell other people how to live until their hearts are open to receiving conviction. When they ask whether something is right or wrong, give them Scripture and let the Holy Spirit do His job. Change from an outside motivation is temporary at best, but once they receive conviction from the Holy Spirit through the Word of truth, their change will become unquestionable.

If the Word said I could do something, I started doing it by faith! Some people would argue that certain gifts were no longer in use by the church, that the devil did not attack us as I supposed, or that people did not have demons inside of them. In regard to those comments, I relayed a Chinese Proverb that says, "Man who say it cannot be done should not interrupt man doing it."[3] I cannot help what others may not understand or are fearful about. I have a charge on my life to walk in obedience to what the Lord has called me. Principles taught in Scripture should work to save, sanctify, and liberate people from darkness so that we can disciple them to multiply and take their positions in the Kingdom. That is the kind of fruit with which I am pleased, and I have seen it produced consistently for many years.

Scripture tool box

Understanding that Scripture has been translated many times over and even paraphrased quite a bit to help those who find it easier to read in more modern language, I try to stay with whatever version is closest to the original languages as a foundation for study. From there, if I want to compare it to other translations or a paraphrase, I can at least know if the translation or paraphrase is keeping the passage consistent to what the author is trying to communicate. From my research, the closest translation to the original languages that I have found is the English Standard Version[4], which I have used throughout this book, except where otherwise noted.

Many people use the extremely popular YouVersion of the Bible, which is an app available for smart phones. A July issue of the New York Times stated about the YouVersion, "Built by LifeChurch.tv, one of the nation's largest and most technologically advanced evangelical churches, YouVersion is part of what the church calls its "digital missions... YouVersion, with over 600 Bible translations in more than 400 languages, is by far the church's biggest success... This month [July, 2013], the app reached 100 million downloads, placing it in the company of technology start-ups like Instagram and Dropbox."[5]

Infallible interpretation

There is only one special revelation from God that man possesses today, and that is the Bible. Scripture states this concept repeatedly and emphatically. The very phrase "It is written" means exclusively transcribed, and not hearsay. We are not to add, nor take away from what is written (Revelation 22:18-19). God's Word is sufficient in itself (Psalm 119:160). It is breathed out by God in written form (2 Timothy 3:15-16). It is inspired (2 Peter 1:20-21). It is what sanctifies us (John 17:17). It, alone, is pure and uncontaminated (Isaiah 8:20). It is not for private interpretation, as the source of interpretation must be from the same pure source as the origin of the Scripture itself (2 Peter 1:20-21). It is only with the Holy Spirit's light that Scripture can be comprehended correctly. The Holy Spirit causes those who are the Lord's to understand Scripture (John 14:16-17, 26).[6]

Qualification for illumination

First Corinthians 4:4 says, "But even if our gospel is veiled, it is veiled to those who are perishing, whose minds the god of this age has blinded, who do not believe, lest the light of the gospel of the glory of Christ, who is the image of God, should shine on them." People need the help of the Holy Spirit to "see" the light of the gospel. Intercession, according to this scripture, can help. As we pray against the darkness and blindness, people can go beyond an intellectual understanding of saving knowledge and go on to make having a moral response to it. I have known people who read the entire Bible and it had no effect on them whatsoever. That was frightening to me. But this happens because, "The natural person does not accept the things of the Spirit of God, for they are folly to him, and he is not able to understand them because they are spiritually discerned" (1 Corinthians 2:14).

Obedience brings blessing

My first goal was to master obedience to the parts of the Bible I did understand and to some extent, I am still there. Some things do not die easily. Some days I still find myself confronting lies. Here is a powerful story. I brought a disastrous issue as a result of my first marriage into my second marriage. It was a life-controlling problem. It was not good, and it is very personal so I will not go into details. For the first five years of my second marriage, it was a real problem. I would go to the altar and pray about it. I would ask people to lay hands on me and pray for me to be healed. It was a deep wound and it was hurting our marriage. One day, the Holy Spirit started speaking to me about a passage of Scripture. He said, "Read that out loud." So I did. He said, "Who wrote that?"

I said, "You did."

He said, "Would I write anything to hurt you?"

I said, "No Sir."

He said, "Do you believe that obedience brings blessing?"

I said, "Yes Sir."

He said, "I know how difficult this if for you, and you do not need to talk any more about it. I know how painful and frightening it is for you when you try to obey this Word. But if you will put your faith in front of your feelings for about two weeks, your obedience will open the floodgate of healing for this. You can trust Me on that."

I said, "Okay. I will try to practice this daily for two weeks Lord."

And so I did. Guess what happened? In two weeks, I was free! Not only was I free, but I have been free ever since. Not only have I been free ever since, but I was able to turn around and help David get free of something too! Simple obedience: read it and do what it says! It works!

When to expand Your search

I wanted to make sure that my spiritual experiences could be found in Scripture. When I read 1 Corinthians 14:34, I thought women were prohibited from teaching the Word of God. Even though I had read through the entire Bible, when I saw this verse, I had a dilemma. Why? It was because God had clearly called me to teach His Word. It was at this time that I had to go back and conduct both a systematic theology search and a biblical theology search. Systematic theology takes into consideration what all the verses are saying about a specific topic such as women in ministry. Biblical theology takes the historical setting into consideration as well. I also had to dig a bit deeper into the original language. Once these two searches are performed and compared, experiences can then be validated or dismissed.

I am not a linguist. When I need to look deeper into the original language of Scripture, I first consult Young's Literal Translation. This translation attempts to preserve the tense and word usage as found in the original Greek and Hebrew writings. It very likely is the most strictly literal English translation ever developed.[7] It would be a difficult read for daily devotions because, as it translates the sentence structure, the sentences do not always make perfect sense in English. However, it does tend to shed some light on passages that seem to be contradictory to the whole counsel of Scripture.

As long as the experiences I had and continue to have are confirmed in Scripture, then I keep going. Spiritual experiences are common all over the world. Some are from God. Some are not. God delights in making Himself known to His children. The question is one of discernment: Who is responsible for the experience – God or satan? First John 4:1 states that we are to "test the spirits to see whether they are from God." Second Corinthians 11:14 states that, "Satan himself masquerades as an angel of light."

An example of this is when once I asked David how I would know whether the answer I heard following an inquiry of the Lord would be His voice or the enemy's voice? He said, "Rebuke it and if it goes away, it is probably the devil because you have authority over him. If the answer continues to return, then go look it up in the Bible. If it is Scripture or it is biblical, then you can be sure that it is God speaking to you. It would also be helpful to ask another trusted Christian if it bears witness with their spirit.

A "biblical" as opposed to "scriptural" confirmation would be, for example, the word "Sunday school" or "Bible school." Those words do not appear in Scripture, but we see that they are "biblical" from Acts 19:9-10, which states about the "*school of Tyrannus*" (KJV), being held for two years in Ephesus where Paul instructed both Greeks and Jews.

If my spiritual experience ever were to exceed my biblical knowledge, I searched further to find it in Scripture and if I could not find it here, I would dig deeper for a confirmation, perhaps in Bible commentaries like *Matthew Henry's Complete Commentary on the Whole Bible* or from early church history. So far, my experiences have yet to exceed what I have found in the pages of Scripture when I read it as the "whole counsel" of God, considering everything from Genesis to Revelation and in context. What I have experienced has and continues not only to line up with Scripture, but is bearing fruit.

Must I know for sure?

Being caught up in biblical debate in the early days of our Bible reading, there were and still are certain topics in Scripture that I am okay with not knowing for sure. For example, although I believe from Scripture that there will be a rapture of the church (1 Corinthians 15:52, 1 Thessalonians 4:16), I am unsure of its timing. I have no idea what was happening when there was silence in heaven (Revelation 8:1). I cannot explain the exact location in the human body from whence a demon exits (Matthew 12:43, Luke 11:24), or if it is rather causing a cathartic experience as it looses the mind, will, and emotions (1 Timothy 2:26). I do know that I have seen some pretty unusual things performed by human bodies that have manifested a demonic spirit. And I have witnessed the shrieks, screams, and writhing on the floor when one is "coming out." My experience has been that when someone is being plagued by a demonic spirit, regardless of its location or how it comes out, they are usually pretty thankful once it is out and the semantics or logistics of how it happens is less important at the time.

I realize that there is a difference between mental illness, anxiety, and demonic oppression. When in doubt, I have a good working relationship with the appropriate licensed professionals who can assist me in determining the best possible solution for an individual. Thankfully, one of the gifts that the Coach manifests through a believer is the discerning of spirits. He is a Master at differentiating between the various needs a person has and gives the minister direction accordingly.

The Main Thing is to Keep the Main Thing the Main Thing

The bottom line for me is this: I want to be caught in the act of living on fire for the Lord and either in preparation for or doing what God has called me to do on this earth to advance the Kingdom of God until He returns. To me, this is the most important thing upon which to focus. You can debate about eschatology and other such spiritual matters as often as you want, as long as you are busy about the Father's business in the process. This is an incredible time to be alive! For me, any time is an incredible time to be alive—as you will see in the book two of the series.

Read the Bible—all of it, and seek God to know Him, to know who you are in Christ, and to walk in step with the Holy Spirit and in obedience to what you read and understand. And know this: you will never grow in your spiritual experience without a step of faith. Hebrews 11:6 states, "… without faith it is impossible to please God, because anyone who comes to him must believe that he exists and that he rewards those who earnestly seek him." Jeremiah 29:13 states, "You will seek me and find me when you seek me with all your heart." I hope you will seek Him more than ever before.

It is a time for the church to be on fire, and not just inside the walls of a building on Sunday. With the increase of fear on so many levels, the increase of mental illness, and the increase of blatant immorality; we had better wake up, grow up, get healed up, and train up this next generation, or we will be facing even more trouble than we see on the increase today. It is always the right time to do what is right. I do not know when the Lord is coming, but I know He IS coming! If you do not cherish the Word of God in your heart, my prayer is that the Coach, through this testimony, will incite you to pick up your sword and get used to holding in your hands and in hiding it in your heart.

See the appendix for some great Bible statistics!

Chapter Five

Personal Application

1. Rate yourself on how often you read and/or study your Bible (1- never, 6 – daily reading, and 10 – devotionally: to find answers and to know God better).
    1 2 3 4 5 6 7 8 9 10

2. Do you read or have you ever considered reading the *One-Year Bible*?   Yes   No

3. What are some advantages of reading the Bible in its entirety?

---

4. What is your greatest challenge in finding time to read your Bible? What can you do to make time if this is your goal?

---

5. Describe how your heart/imagination sees God the Father.

---

6. Could you relate to the point made that there are beliefs so strong in us, that at times, they can keep us from progressing spiritually? Write about your own experience.

---

7. Are you a vessel ready to fulfill a higher purpose or one who is still bound in a cycle of sin, old wounds, lies, unbelief, and unforgiveness?

---

8. Are you allowing ignorance to keep you from walking in victory over darkness? If that is true, what can you do to change that fact?

_____

_____

9. If you have been a Christian for more than a year, how is your ability to hear God's voice better now than it was when you first received Christ? How can you improve your ability to hear God's voice?

_____

_____

10. Do you believe the Bible is true and is the infallible Word of God? Yes   No
Why or why not?

_____

_____

11. If you are struggling in an area of obedience to God, can you think of a Scripture or two that you could stretch out your faith upon for a breakthrough?
List them.

_____

_____

12. When Jesus returns, what do you want to be "caught in the act" doing?

_____

_____

13. After reading this chapter, what might be a "next right step" for you?

_____

_____

In closing

Heavenly Father, You are a wonderful provider. We love You and appreciate the Words of truth which You have given us so that we can know You. We are amazed at the lengths to which You would go out of love for us. Thank You Father, that Your Word divides our soul from our spirit, and it heals us. Your Word brings comfort in that it gives us the assurance that You are interacting with us on a daily basis. Your Word challenges us to keep our eyes on Jesus, the author and perfecter of our faith. Our focus upon Him frees us from having to focus on our sin and our weakness. We thank You for the freedom we enjoy to own and read the Word of God. We pray for Your supernatural provision for all those who hunger after Your Word and do not have access to a Bible. Make a way where there is no seeming way, Father! We agree that this will continuously happen until the day of Your return so that all may know Christ! We choose to fast so that we may create more room for Your Word in our hearts and minds. May we be increasingly faithful to the study of Your Word and be instant in season to give a reason for the hope that we have in You. Pour Your love through us Father, so that we may share that love with others, showing how much we care before we show how much we know about the gospel. We desire a genuine faith built upon the foundation of Your truth. Set Yourself as a seal upon our hearts and may we ever live to bring glory and honor to Your Name and the Name of Your precious Son. We pray this together in the lovely Name of Jesus. Amen.

Chapter Six

FREEDOM FROM GENERATIONAL SINS

For you know that it was not with perishable things such as silver or gold that you were redeemed from the empty way of life handed down to you from your ancestors (1 Peter 1:18).

Years ago, Hank Williams Jr. recorded a song called, *Family Tradition*. The chorus poses a series of rhetorical questions asked by various persons in the singer's life.

"I am very proud of my daddy's name
All though his kind of music and mine ain't exactly the same.
Stop and think it over. Put yourself in my position.
If I get stoned and sing all night long it's a family tradition.
Hank, why do you drink? Why do you roll smoke?
Why must you live out the songs that you wrote?
Stop and think it over, try and put yourself in my unique position.
If I get stoned and sing all night long, it's a family tradition!"[1]

What was he trying to tell us? He was saying, "Like father, like son." Through his lyrics, Williams beautifully described what we know as generational sin patterns.

Sometimes families boast about how their kids take after them; others lament. Today, I understand that God created me to be a leader, and to be strong. However, the enemy used my circumstances in tandem with my own family traditions to make me tough. He exaggerated my strength. I have met many people who were tough or even bullies when, in reality, they were very fearful.

As the enemy breaks you down with rejection, abandonment, trauma, and so on, the first thing he wants is your faith. He is trying to prove that God is not good in hopes that you will toss your faith aside. If he finds that he cannot steal your faith, he will go after your weaknesses. If your weaknesses are well guarded, he will launch an attack to exaggerate your strengths. I believe the way that he is able to do this is because your strengths become the easiest hiding place for your pain and typically, we do not guard our strengths.

When your strengths are exaggerated, some people will like you more, while others may become overwhelmed by you. You may feel misunderstood, judged, and disliked, or you might launch a successful career! Either way, your strengths are still your strengths. They are not wrong. They are God-given. They may be exaggerated and a bit annoying, but once you are healed, you will find your balance. Just pray and prepare, because some people will remember you as you were when you made the largest impression, whether you were entertaining or offensive. They will find it challenging to see you or accept you as any other way than who you were before you found the real you.

Being tough was what my grandparents' and my parents' generations did quite naturally in challenging or oppressive circumstances. Emotional pain was not something our families were accustomed to resolving. Dad used to call me, "Chip off the ole' block." In fact, he said that I was, "Tough as a pine knot and had hair like steel wool." My hair was NEVER like steel wool, but I am sure you get the point. Growing up for my parents and for me was tough, and thus we just grew another layer of skin and kept going.

Interestingly, once David and I were married, the only way he could make me cry was when he said, "You are a hard woman, Monica Ann!" Mama called me Monica Ann when I was in trouble. I never dreamed I would have a husband who would say it! Two generations taught me to get tough. Being tough was who we were. Being tough was what we did. We were tough and proud of it! Life taught me to get even more tough, particularly if I was pushed, once I left home. That did not work out for me so well.

When I look back into my family tree, and I know we can all probably say this, I see sin patterns repeated over and over again. I do not know if anyone is exempt from that cycle. Children learn things even when they are not intentionally taught. Realistically, as parents, like the Apostle Paul, we all struggle at times with doing what is right (Romans 7).

Line of Demarcation

One of the generational sins trying to take hold of me was to "just to keep going" in life's defining moments. Regardless of what happens to you, just keep going. Do not talk about it. Do not change your behavior. Pull yourself together. Get busier if necessary, but do NOT acknowledge how that moment affected you—because it did. It always does and it should.

In my second year of a second chance in marriage, as I was nearing the end of the second reading of the *One-Year Bible*, I was convicted by something I read. I do not know if it was a particular passage or if it was the entire message, but I finally responded to a defining moment. I resolved something in my heart that sounded like this: "I do not know how Lord, but the buck stops here!" That moment was so strong for me that I not only felt resolve coming from my heart, it also came out of my mouth. It became a declaration and when I spoke those words out loud, both my intellect and my enemy heard the resolve in my words.

Without knowing details or having anyone to explain it more clearly, besides the experience I had with the lady in the crowd that day, I knew that the Lord had a particular path He wanted me to follow the rest of my days on the earth. I realized from Scripture that, while God would not take away my personality, some of the coping mechanisms and the masks I wore to cover up what was unresolved would have to go. I had no idea what would be the first step. To me, it was daunting to even think about what it would take, but my desire to obey God was growing. I was alive for a reason. I had a destiny, and I knew I could not achieve it in the condition I was in at that time. Sometimes, I still felt like I had chains around my heart. However, God was beginning to break down my defenses. I needed to know Him more intimately in order to feel safe enough surrendering to the level of vulnerability necessary for my complete deliverance and healing.

The Coach was speaking in that moment volumes, although I did not hear the words conversationally. He was showing me that God's love was real and it was truly in my heart. Life is full of defining moments: places where the love of God beckons you to stop and make a choice for life instead of death. I had already experienced many of those moments. In spite of the silence of my grandparents, I loved them and was able to receive love from them. In spite of the harshness of my grandfather, I noticed love in his gentle smile, especially when we were out feeding rabbits and chickens together. In spite of being the butt of insensitive comments at school, I wanted to be available to pray for and to help my peers. In spite of being a young, lonely wife, my heart ached more for the lonely and broken in the housing projects of Nashville. There are intersections in life where you have a choice to become bitter or to extend grace and to make life better. Whether anyone noticed, and I for one did not, God was keeping me on the course of extending grace. He had His hand on my heart, protecting the innocence of my child-like faith, refocusing me on matters of life as death tried to hold my attention. My defining moments were redemptive in a way that I did not perceive "in the moment." They became memories about the loving character of God.

What on Earth is going on Inside of Me?

How can we allow life's traumas to keep us so fearful and guarded in most of our moments and yet have other moments of being boldly ourselves? How can we be so loving and kind in certain circumstances, like me or even my grandfather, and yet be so arrogant or hateful in other circumstances? I believe the answer can be found in what I call, "the do-do chapter," or Romans Chapter Seven. In this chapter, the Apostle Paul states that whenever he was confronted by a commandment in the law, sin rose up and took the reins of his beliefs and, thus, his behavior. As a result, what he wanted to do, he could not do and what he did not want to do, he was seemingly powerless to stop. He explained that this did not make the law bad, but rather it exposed sin as being what it is: a life controlling part of our fleshly, human nature. It is something from which we cannot separate ourselves and is a part of us to which the enemy has continuous access. You can no more cut away your flesh than you can remove your vital organs and survive. That is why Scripture gives us exhortations such as to take our thoughts captive to the obedience of Christ when hell makes their suggestions (2 Corinthians 10:4-5), to submit and to surrender to Christ and His finished work in all situations of life (Ephesians 5:20-22; 25, Ephesians 6:1, 5, 9; Colossians 2:20, Galatians 5:1), and my favorite, to keep our eyes on Christ at all times (Hebrews 12), because that which holds your focus is what will have authority over your beliefs, and thus your behavior (Proverbs 23:7).

If the Holy Spirit, is in you, then good is at work in you because God is the only one who is "good" by definition (Mark 10:18). When you yield to Him, you are yielding to the "good works" He has planned from the beginning to do through you (Ephesians 2:10).

Even when the Holy Spirit does not reside in a person, humanity is still created in the image of God, however darkened by the curse of sin. For those without the lamp of God burning inside their hearts, there can be moments of benevolence, kindness, generosity, and the like. However, these moments are motivated out of need and not an expression from the One who defines unconditional love.

Becoming focused on Jesus would define my journey over the course of the next two seasons of my life. I had plenty inside of me that was fighting for my attention. However, the next several years, for me, would begin to shed light upon the enemy's scheme. In what may be His finest moment in my life, God would set him up and then valiantly take him down from the throne he had established over my body and soul. Sadly, you must wait until the next book to read that incredible story. I do, however want to share a few insights about breaking generational sin patterns so that you are freer to enjoy your relationship with the Lord as well as others.

Much Ado about Generational Sin

Generational sin grows the longer you hold on to it. If you do not deal with it, your kids are probably going to act just like you. When you begin to see yourself in them, it is possible that you find yourself treating them harshly. In so doing, you are actually punishing in them what you do not like about yourself. I know that sounds horrible and I am sure that you probably have a great deal of wonderful characteristics to pass on to your children, but some of you understand what I am talking about.

Here are a few examples of the indicators of a generational sin pattern:

"Our family is full of people who divorce when the going gets tough. I was not surprised when it happened to me."

"I struggle with anxiety. But, my mama had anxiety. Her mama had anxiety, and her mama's daddy committed suicide."

"My great-grandma had cancer. My grandma had cancer. My dad had cancer, and I fear that I will probably get cancer somewhere down the road."

Generational sin reminds me of the Japanese *Bonzai* tree. As the trees grow and begin to sprout branches, the designer can put little weights on each branch to bend it in a specific direction or shape. In like manner, our families' traits and generational sins can weigh upon us and make us inclined toward those behaviors that, in turn, get passed down to our children and grandchildren.

As you have seen from my story, family traits, good and bad, can be passed down to the next generation. One of the great blessings that came out of my family was the strength to survive! Generational blessings or sins both shape our beliefs and thus, our behavior. This is another reason why we need to renew our minds by reading and applying God's Word.

Generational Sin Patterns – What They are Not

Some people refer to a generational sin pattern as a generational curse, and that being something stronger than themselves that keeps them from breaking free. The verses Exodus 20:5b and 34:7 state how God will punish the iniquity of the fathers unto the children all the way to the third and fourth generations of those that hate Him, or do not honor Him. The explanation of a generational curse is, in some circles, that God will allow the consequences as well as demonic forces to operate in the lives of those carrying the curse. That is very true for people who have not received Christ because they are all under the curse of the Law (Galatians 3:10-13). However, can a Christian have a generational curse? What does this mean? It is something that I have been grappling with for a long time, both for the sake of my own freedom as well as to help others. After careful study and helping people break generational sin patterns over the years, here is my conclusion.

Simply put, God allows the children, to four generations of those who do not obey Him, to reap the consequences of a families' sin. However, if within those generations, no one comes to Christ, the cycle continues on down the generational line. For example, if a mother mistreats her body with drugs and alcohol, her newborn baby may be born with fetal alcohol syndrome. This is the spiritual law of sowing and reaping working in tandem with the consequences of the mother's behavior. Some look at a situation like that one and say, "How could God allow that?" That is easy. Sin has consequences, and it carries death within it. Tragically, people who sow in sinful disobedience will likely reap the consequences, not only in their own life, but also in their progeny.

The threat of these same sins being passed on to a generation beyond the first will depend upon the children's choices, whether or not to follow the sins of their parents. It is unfortunate that the children of parents who pass on these generational sin patterns may not recognize their need for change before they have children of their own. Thus, the cycle continues, passing the same sinful patterns on to the children's children.

We know through the whole counsel of Scripture that children are not actually "punished" by God for the sins of a parent. Ezekiel 18:20 clearly states,

> "The soul who sins shall die. The son shall not suffer for the iniquity of the father, nor the father suffer for the iniquity of the son. The righteousness of the righteous shall be upon himself, and the wickedness of the wicked shall be upon himself."

That verse tells me that the children of those how do not obey God and have even passed their sinful traits down, those children have a chance! These children may be struggling with the consequences of sowing and reaping, but if they accept the Lord and are sincerely walking with Him, regardless of where they are in the process, He is going to enlighten them, convict them, and give them the grace to break that cycle. I know this is true. I deal with it in counseling all the time.

This brings us back to the question: Can a Christian remain under a curse? There is only one curse, and that is the curse of sin. The Old Testament does say in various places, "Cursed is the man who…", but again, there was no grace in operation at the time. Therefore, at any given time, if you happened to be between sacrifices, you could disobey the vast array of laws and fall under "the curse of sin." But now that Christ has died, if someone is under the curse of sin, then they are not truly born again. We know this by Galatians 3:10-13, which states,

> "For all who rely on works of the law are under a curse; for it is written, 'Cursed be everyone who does not abide by all things written in the Book of the Law, and do them.' Now it is evident that no one is justified before God by the law, for 'The righteous shall live by faith.' But the law is not of faith, rather 'The one who does them shall live by them.' Christ redeemed us from the curse of the law by becoming a curse for us—for it is written, 'Cursed is everyone who is hanged on a tree.'"

Second Corinthians 13:5 warns, "Examine yourselves, to see whether you are in the faith. Test yourselves. Or do you not realize this about yourselves, that Jesus Christ is in you?—unless indeed you fail to meet the test!"

Spells, Hexes, and Curses

Can someone, like a witch, put a curse on a Christian? Is that the same as a curse of sin?

The Word of God states in Proverbs 26:2, "Like a fluttering sparrow or a darting swallow, an undeserved curse does not come to rest."

The one who utters a curse against you because they are angry at you or they do not like you–because you are under the protection of the blood of Christ–is ineffective. The Bible states that, like a fluttering sparrow or a darting swallow, both of which return right back from whence they came, that curse will also go back from whence it came. Let me give you an example.

A friend of mine was a registered nurse. She came back on shift after a few days off and discovered that the other nurses were talking really negative and saying bad things were going to happen to them in the days ahead. When my friend questioned this line of reasoning, they said that one of the patients had been telling their fortunes.

My friend, now back on duty, had this woman as a patient. She went in to check on her, take her vitals, and so on. The patient tried to open up a dialogue with my friend as to her future. However, my friend being a Christian, said, "I already know my future. In fact, God has promised me a great hope and future." The patient persisted to say bad things over my friend but each time, she refuted it with truth.

Soon, my friend was off work again for a few more days. When she went back to work again, she found that this patient was still there and was, in fact, worse than before. When my friend went in to check on her this time, she said something such as, "My goodness, what is going on with you? I thought you would be well and gone by now."

The patient looked at her and said, "I will tell you what is going on with me. When you would not allow me to tell your fortune, I put a curse on you. However, instead of hurting you, as I see you are just fine, everything I cursed you with has come back on me."

In Luke 10:19, Jesus said, "Behold, I have given you authority to tread on serpents and scorpions, and over all the power of the enemy, and nothing shall hurt you." Some might argue that this promise was given to the original disciples and before the victory of the cross. True enough! So think about what power has been extended to us, who are disciples today after He defeated death and hell, was given all authority, and is now seated at the right hand of the Father making intercession for every situation we face! There is POWER over the undeserved curses that are cast about today.

I will never forget, years ago when I managed a pet store, one of our employees was a Wiccan. I loved this woman and her son, who also worked for us. We had many great conversations. One day, she was sitting in the office, and I was walking by the office door, when she said, "I perceive that you have a lot of power."

I said, "Thanks for saying that, it is really encouraging. But that is Him, not me."

Technically, I do not believe that generational curses are spiritual punishments from God by way of demonic attacks that we are opened up to through the sins of prior generations. I still believe that the generational curse spoken of in Exodus 20 and 34 is the curse of sin, broken by Christ's work on the cross, and that it produces the consequences of the law of sowing and reaping.

All men are subject to physical laws as well as spiritual laws. Galatians 6:7-8 states,

> "Do not be deceived: God is not mocked, for whatever one sows, that will he also reap. For the one who sows to his own flesh will from the flesh reap corruption, but the one who sows to the Spirit will from the Spirit reap eternal life."

However, if you are walking in the Spirit, you will not fulfill the lusts of the flesh and thus, you will not reap negative consequences. Keeping your eyes off of yourself and on Jesus has so many benefits!

I Have Great News for You

If you are truly born again, nothing about your old life can stick or remain permanent any longer. You are not who you used to be because 2 Corinthians 5:17 states that those who are in Christ are new creations! You are a new creation because now, Someone more powerful than yourself has come to live inside of you: the Kingdom Coach. If you truly love and are grateful for what Christ did, then you will want to follow Him in a life of obedience. That means that as you study the Word of God, your mind will become renewed. All of the fleshly remains of your old life will be sanctified as you quit believing what you used to believe and learn how to live according to spiritual truth. As you read the Bible and as you allow it to read you, the truth will change your beliefs. Consequently, your behavior and, moreover, your consequences will also change.

Galatians 3:27-28 further states, "for all of you who were baptized into Christ have clothed yourselves with Christ. There is neither Jew nor Gentile, neither slave nor free, nor is there male and female, for you are all one in Christ Jesus." Once you became born again, you were crucified, buried, and raised up with Christ, and now you are in Christ. In Him, according to this scripture, you are now neither elevated above nor considered below anyone else in Christ. You left your current state of position and became part of a Kingdom. You gave up your nationality, your status in this life, and even any issues with gender inequality. I would also add that you probably fell out of your family tree as well. While that does not mean that you are no longer part of your precious family (as all are precious image bearers and have redemptive value), it merely means that you are no longer subject to being "held" by the sinful tendencies of your family line.

Caution: Demonic Oppression

Here is the caveat. As a Christian, you are already healed in spirit (Isaiah 53:5). But the Bible promises us healing for the soul and the body (Psalm 103:3, 1 Thessalonians 5:23). What if the enemy can tempt you to believe something that is not true YET, and by refusing to cast that vain imagination down, you succumb to that very fear and reap destruction? Can that happen? Sure it can, and it does. Generationally, you may have been taught to fear and even accept things yet to occur. But, remember, you are supposed to be on your way to renewing your mind anyway. How can you walk in obedience to your response to the great commission (Matthew 28:20) to obey everything Christ commanded if you are not reading your Bible? If you are in neutral, going nowhere spiritually, you are a sitting duck to the enemy, and that is your choice. It may be a generational sin pattern, but it is your current choice to sin. James 4:17 states, "So whoever knows the right thing to do and fails to do it, for him it is sin."

If we are born again, but continue to repeat the generational sins of our family after we have been convicted of them, it is a sin of commission. Likewise, if we are born again, but continue in generational sin by remaining in our ignorance to the truth in the Word of God, then we are committing a sin of omission. Either way, we have believed a lie or we are ignorant about our sin and/or about the promises of God. For me, the lie was that being tough was not just okay, it was admirable. I had to come to terms with the fact that lacking gentleness was a sin and an unwillingness to yield to the fruit that only the Holy Spirit could express. What amazing provision the Father made possible for us! I did not have to solve the problem of being tough by myself. I did not have to DO anything because it was beyond my power to resolve the issue on my own.

The overwhelming circumstances of life cause us to erect walls to protect ourselves. Naturally, we grow tired of being a push-over and we easily become calloused, tough, or insensitive. However, as we come to the saving knowledge of Jesus Christ, we must realize a few things: Firstly, we cannot solve our own problems. The painful consequences of sin in our world require the power to cleanse and to heal that only a relationship with the Savior can provide. Secondly, idolizing any family trait when it causes someone else to stumble is sin. Thirdly, when we recognize a behavior that is opposite to the fruit of the Spirit, we must surrender that behavior through repentance. Finally, we receive healing for our pain and yield to the Spirit, who has the ability to express what we cannot. If we do not pursue this redemptive process when we are convicted by the Holy Spirit in regard to these and other generational sins, then we will suffer the consequences.

It is in this way that we "come under a curse," which is not the curse of sin, but the natural consequences of the sin. Even if you are born again, if you do not pursue sanctification through an increasing knowledge of the Word of God, and you continue in sin, you may still be God's child, but the doors are flung open to the enemy because he is a legalist who is looking for a loophole. That is not God's fault. He has already done everything He needed to do to secure your victory through His Son's victory.

This, once again, is a matter of your beliefs. By your rebellion or ignorance, you are refusing to receive something from God that would help you break a pattern of "stinking thinking."

You could believe that because Grandma and Mama had mental illness that you will also have mental illness, instead of confessing that you have the mind of Christ.

You could believe that you are going to get cancer because it is swimming around in your gene pool instead of believing that healing was in the atonement and that God still heals today (as I am living proof!) In fact, you could end up worrying about it to the point that your immune system weakens and you succumb to the disease or a spirit of the disease (more about that in the next book).

Your beliefs not only save you, they keep you. But your beliefs can also come into agreement with the enemy's plan to steal, kill, and destroy you. That is why it is so important to know who you are in Christ and know what you believe – and know that what you believe is what God says.

Simply put, demonic oppression can result from generational sin patterns that "run in the family" IF the children of the family continue to walk in CURRENT sinful choices after they are born again.

In Luke 6:40, Jesus said, "A student is not above his teacher, but everyone who is fully trained will be like his teacher." And Peter said in 1 Peter 1:18, "You were redeemed from the empty way of life handed down to you from your forefathers." There are powerful influences upon your life during your formative years, but you are not bound to the resulting consequences of walking in the beliefs or behaviors that are ungodly for the rest of your life. The enemy will tempt you the same way he tempted your former generations to cope and defend, instead of casting their cares on God. But you can operate in more wisdom as you immerse yourself in God's Word.

Freedom is Around the Corner

Here is where it gets exciting! After you have asked the Lord's help to identify these generational sin patterns, and after you have repented of them, forgiven your ancestors for their influence, renounced the power of the enemy, and applied the truth to the new habit patterns you want to enjoy, you then are also able to begin interceding for those who are still alive in the generations past. God will raise you up as the "white sheep" of the family and open hearts and doors for you to minister reconciliation to family members in need—even those with whom you have been estranged. I have seen this happen so many times. It is how you partner with Christ in destroying the work of the enemy. It is one of your first priorities in preparing to walk in your authority as deputy sheriff on the earth!

Anything that remains in the dark belongs to the devil. If this chapter has spoken to you about your need to identify and break generational sin, you can do it right now. Get these things out into the open, hold yourself accountable, and stop the enemy from tormenting you and your precious family.

A question I get asked quite often is: "Monica, can a Christian have a demon?" I simply say, "You can have as many as you are willing to tolerate." In my own story, at the point in history relayed in this book, I still had much demonic opposition to face. I did not know of or trust anyone who had developed tools to help me. God used my ignorance and mistrust to keep my eyes on Him, leading me to my own healing, and training me to do what I do today. However, you can use the tools provided in this book series and start discovering and enjoying your own personal freedom! We have seen them work for numerous people over the last several years.

Chapter Six

Personal Application

1. What will the enemy do if he cannot steal your faith and when your weaknesses are well guarded?

___

2. Do you believe that you are able to fulfill your destiny in your present condition? What do you need to keep moving forward?
   - ☐ I need healing from past, unresolved issues
   - ☐ I need to break some generational sin patterns
   - ☐ I need more discipleship

3. List one example of a generational sin pattern at work.

___

4. List a generational blessing that has been passed onto you by your family.

___

5. What scripture tells us that God will hold each family member responsible for no one else's sin but their own?

___

6. What scripture tells us that a Christian cannot be under the curse of the law?

___

7. What scripture tells us that, as Christians, we are not subject to an undeserved curse as a form of retaliation?

___

8. What scripture talks about the law of sowing and reaping?

___

Freedom from Generational Sins

9. What scripture verifies that we are no longer controlled by our family tree?

_____

10. What is the proper response to the great commission of Matthew 28:19-20?

_____

11. If you are a Christian, how do you keep from coming under the consequences of sin?

_____

If you would like, take a moment to pray and ask the Lord to help you identify the generational sin patterns in your life. Here is how:
a) On page 171, put a check by any sin pattern already listed or fill in the blanks with other sin patterns that the Holy Spirit illuminates
b) Write the person's name in the blank that was the greatest influence of that sin pattern in your life.
c) As you pray through the prayer that follows, be sure to forgive those who had the most influence over your life in each area.
d) Pray through the prayer for each sin individually.
e) Meditate on the scriptures provided for each issue and find others that you need to renew your mind about these issues, to help reinforce the boundary line you are setting against these patterns and to encourage you to walk in freedom.

How this works

Simply, it is bringing yourself into personal accountability. Everything we do, we do by faith. This is merely a tool to help you work through the process completely and according to the Word of God. You are humbling yourself by admitting that you have these issues, thus opening yourself up for God's divine power to do the work of sanctification in you. You are partnering with the work of the Holy Spirit through Christ to free you from these issues. You are renouncing any work of darkness in your life. Hopefully, you will be seeking the Lord through the Scriptures to renew your mind in regard to what to believe about each issue and so that you have a sword to swing when the enemy comes to test your freedom (Luke 4:13).

GENERATIONAL SINS MINISTRY WORKSHEET

Generational Sin Pattern	Influence	Scripture Reference
stubborn independence	Adam & Eve	Ps. 32:9-10, Prov. 16:18
sinful anger	_____	Eph 4:26, 31; James 1:20
abuse (physical, sexual, verbal, etc.)	_____	Matt. 7:12, James 1:19-20
argumentativeness	_____	Phil. 2:14
critical/harsh words	_____	Eph. 4:29
dominance & superiority	_____	Gal. 3:28
racism	_____	Acts 10:28, 34-35
materialism	_____	Heb. 13:5, Eccl. 5:10
addictive behavior	_____	Rom. 6:16, 1 Cor. 6:12
mental instability	_____	2 Tim. 1:7, Luke 1:37, 1 Cor. 14:13
propensity to illness	_____	3 John 1:2, Ps. 103:3 Prov. 17:22
divorce	_____	Mal. 2:14-15, Mt. 19:8-9
_____	_____	
_____	_____	
_____	_____	

Freedom Prayer

Pray through this prayer for each of the issues and corresponding persons you checked or listed.

> **Thank you, Holy Spirit, for helping me to identify the generational sin patterns that have dominated my life. By faith, Father, I am placing my trust in the Divine power that raised Christ from the dead to do what I cannot do as I place these things before You.**
>
> **In the Name of Jesus, I renounce _____.**
> **I ask You to forgive me for anytime I have already given in to this generational sin. I break the power of the enemy by the authority You have given me as a believer. I plead the precious and powerful blood of Jesus over my life and I receive cleansing from this pattern of sin and the resulting bondage over my life.**
>
> **By the power of the grace and forgiveness You have given me, I now forgive _____ for their negative influence on my life. I release them to You to do a work in them that only You can do. Bless them Lord as only You can. Show me any opportunity for reconciliation possible either now or in the future and give me the grace and wisdom to follow Your lead and to not do it on my own.**
>
> **I ask that You would clearly show me the way of escape if I am tempted to pick up these sin patterns again. Give me ears to hear You when the Holy Spirit convicts me. Remind me of the Word that is hidden in my heart so that I may be ready when the enemy tries to test my freedom. I pray all this in the wonderful Name above all Names – Jesus, You are my King and I give you all the glory for the victory in my life today! Amen.**

Chapter Seven

THE FREEDOM OF FORGIVENESS

"Bear with each other and forgive one another if any of you has a grievance against someone. Forgive as the Lord forgave you" **(Colossians 3:13).**

I want to begin this chapter by giving honor and glory to the Lord. As this entire book has been mostly centered on the work of the Holy Spirit, our Kingdom Coach, we must recognize that He is the Spirit of Christ. The Holy Spirit is the One who keeps us connected to the Father's heart and the words, work, and intercession of Jesus Christ. It is in Christ that we find the strength to not only forgive others, but also to walk in a spirit of forgiveness.

I am grateful that Jesus saved my life. I passed from death to eternal life and from physically dying to an abundant, healthy life because of the power in His life! He is my elder brother, my Lord, and my King. I have found my greatest joy in serving Him.

Here is a montage of Scripture to sum up the incredible life that is found in Him! "The 'Word of God' (Jesus Christ) became incarnate (John 1:14). 'In Him was life' (John 1:4). He proclaimed that He was 'the way, the truth and the life' (John 14:6), and that He 'had come that we might have His life' (John

10:10). 'Whoever believes in the Son has the eternal life' of Jesus Christ (John 3:16, 36). 'He who has the Son has the life' (I John 5:12), and has 'passed out of death into life' (I John 3:14). 'The Spirit (of Christ) gives life (II Cor. 3:6), whereby the Christian can 'walk in newness of life' (Rom. 6:4), 'reign in life through Jesus Christ' (Rom. 5:17), and be 'saved by His life' (Rom. 5:10). Because Jesus Christ rose from the dead unto life, the Christian can 'pass out of death into life' (I John 3:14), that by being 'born of God' (I John 4:7; John 1:13), 'born of the Spirit' of Christ (John 3:6,8), 'born from above' (John 3:3,7). 'He saved us...by the washing of regeneration and renewing by the Holy Spirit' (Titus 3:5). He is the living Word (1 John 1:1-2) which sanctifies us (1 Corinthians 1:30)."[1]

Never Let Them See You Sweat!

While I was busy getting the Word of God into my heart, I still had closets full of wrong beliefs and unbelief locked inside the painful memories of my soul. I remember sometimes I would accidentally hit my head on the corner of a cabinet door that I had forgotten to shut. I would cry every time, not because it hurt so badly, as the protective plate that replaced my skull is quite sturdy. It was my bruised emotions that were always triggered from the accident and from the day that kid took off my helmet and hit me in the head.

In order to conduct ministry most effectively, I kept the rooms of my soul locked up tight. Were we not supposed to have it all together? Only my husband and the Coach had access to those locked rooms, although David did not venture there on too many occasions. He was busy working through his own issues of self-worth and making a living.

Other than the Coach, I was afraid to allow anyone to see how much pain I truly carried. I still did not want to think about it or even talk about it. I was, however, enjoying the Word, and He continued to illuminate passages in the Word that were very encouraging. The promises of God's Word were slowly increasing my peace, one layer at a time.

Sometimes ministry leaders hide their unresolved issues. They may be in denial. They may be too busy. They may fear judgment from the people. Regardless of the reason they hide, if they fall, the Body of Christ gets hurt, discouraged, and disillusioned. God will give leaders plenty of opportunities to come clean on their own, but if they do not, exposure will eventually occur. When it does, it is a merciful gift. God will allow it in order to protect the Body of Christ from even greater injury. Many times, the pain of falling becomes the impetus for leaders to heal and to slowly make their way back to the former and even greater positions of authority, but with more strength, wisdom, and greater humility.

The lost, in particular, point the finger at the fallen leaders who appeared to be holy, particularly if they spoke out harshly about others who were in sin. But is it not our lack of vulnerability and transparency that causes people to react that way? If leaders are transparent about how they have struggled and have overcome, if they ask for prayer like anyone else when they have a need, and if they step down if and when a current struggle is bearing weight on their leadership, would the body and the lost not see it as less discouraging or offensive? I have seen this beautiful transparency among the leaders with whom we serve today. For the most part, it is a healthy, balanced body, and it is a joy to serve there.

Chinks in My Armor

I went from being suppressed by circumstances as a young girl, to silently blossoming into the leader I was meant to become. Of course, the enemy had deceived me into taking the longer route and the harder path.

In the earlier years, when I left home, I was an only child in a big city. I knew no one besides my first husband and his family, and at first, I barely knew them or him! I had no college education. I had to survive. I had to find work. I did not even know how to dress for an interview. I used every gift and strength I had to present myself as an asset or a blessing, which was a challenge for me since I struggled to believe it myself. I mustered as much chutzpah as possible, both in the secular world where I worked and in the ministry. People were needy and someone had to do something about it! The beautiful thing about it all was that I can see how God even used my immature zeal back then to prepare me for what I would do years later.

When God is working on taking you from the church to the Kingdom (and I will talk more about that in the second book), He does not waste anything. He is the only one who can reach down into your mess and pull out something beautiful. That is why, today, we train people and help them grow in character, but we should never throw their zeal out the window. The Bible says not to put out the Spirit's fire (1 Thessalonians 5:19). People are on a journey. If you have something valuable to add to it, ask God to open that door to their heart. Add something beautiful and strong to the passion they already possess.

In later years, I thought everyone wanted to know what I discovered. That was not true. No matter how much you know, if someone is not asking for your advice, keep it to yourself, or write a book! It would take me years of walking with the Coach to learn the grace, mercy, self-control, and gentleness it would take to do what I do today. But remember, I had a great deal of junk to unpack. Today, the Lord has helped me develop many tools that help people move into freedom much faster than I.

Crowds have never bothered me; however I find that I am much more content being quiet in a crowd unless I have a task to perform. If I am leading or hosting, I am very comfortable do so. If I am not, I am very comfortable being still unless I have something relevant to share. Having a quiet nature, and being alone for the majority of my years growing up, it is very easy for me to be "alone" in a crowd. Feeling invisible for so long is, at first, somewhat painful. But once you resolve the identity issues it breeds, it can result in tremendous productivity! I can do movies, dinner, shopping, and many other things by myself and have a great time being quietly content or to use that time for study. However, it is also not unusual for me to meet and talk to several people in so doing.

In earlier days, being a typical only child, I focused on myself quite a bit. Therefore, if I had tasks to complete, it was very easy for me to focus completely on the task and not on people. Let me give you an example. Years ago, during a season when I had multiple administrative responsibilities at church, I discovered that I was ignoring people. I would not have known this except for a dear lady who brought it to my attention one night in a prayer line. I admire her because she came to tell me out of obedience in order to offer me forgiveness. I had been too focused on my tasks to notice her one evening, and it hurt her feelings. You never know what people are going through. Something that we could care less about one day may really hurt us the next, depending on the daily challenges we face. I have to admit that my first reaction to her was, "Really?" I apologized as sincerely as I was able, but I was still a bit tough. I had yet to go through the redemptive process I described in the last chapter. I had yet to receive that revelation for myself. Yielding to that process makes all the difference in how you react or respond to people. Thanks to John Maxwell, I learned that leaders must "walk slowly through the crowd."[2] People are more important than tasks.

I am quite certain that I hurt or offended many more than the one who came to tell me about it. Throughout my healing process, as the Coach would bring situations to my mind where my actions were hurtful or negligent to people, I tried to go back and make it right with them. Romans 12:18 gives exhortation, "So far as it depends on you, live peaceably with all." If you are reading this book and you are one of those that I either hurt or ignored, please know I am sorry for anything I did to cause you to stumble. I mean that with all of my heart.

The important point of making things right once you discover that you have done others wrong is this: You get out of a personal prison by making things right with those you have hurt and by forgiving those who have hurt you. That is the power of forgiveness.

The Reward of Forgiveness

It is hard to move on with loose ends. You cannot make the people you have hurt or the people who have hurt or neglected you come to peace with you, but you can pray for them. You can also take the initiative to forgive. When we are obedient to take steps the Father says we should take, where our natural actions end, His supernatural activity begins. Obedience tends to rain down blessings on the offender and the offended.

I have led many people through an exercise of forgiveness for over ten years in freedom weekends—a three day conference my husband and I have been doing since 2004. I have sat with countless individuals in my counseling office and taken them through this exercise as well. More than several times, I have seen an interesting phenomenon take place. When people choose to forgive someone who has hurt them in the past, it is not uncommon for those very people to end up calling them or showing up on their doorstep soon thereafter. They call or come to make peace. It is as though when an act of forgiveness is taken and peace unlocks the prison the victim was in, there is also a supernatural grace that goes out to the offender, somehow breaking chains off of them also so that they might reach out to make amends.

I do not know if I realized it was happening until I looked back. When I surrendered my life and committed to allow God to heal me, I also prayed that He would redeem my past. It had not been that long since I left home, just seven years, and it had not been long at all since I was in my first marriage, less than a year. I know that I prayed a very general prayer to forgive those in the past who had hurt me, whether intentionally or unintentionally, but my heart was very sincere at this time. I had a strong sense that I only had a certain amount of time to get things right. That prayer released grace all around us.

Once David and I were married, he gave up his old sweat lodge and I moved out of the house my parents and I had built together. Now that I think of it, building that home with my folks was very redemptive because the construction industry had taken my dad away from home for long hours from the time I was seven years old until I married at seventeen. Building this home was a project that enabled us to spend lots of time together and it was fun. We all enjoyed it. I lived in it for four years while my parents traveled for my dad to inspect nuclear power plants – a job he went back to school for after the construction industry bottomed out in 1980. After he decided to leave that industry and settle in Tennessee, they returned to the home we had built.

I remember one afternoon, David and I were visiting my folks. I was sitting in the dining room with my dad, and we were talking about how glad he was for David and me. Through the course of the conversation, with tears he began to talk about how sorry he was that he did not step in and do more to stop me from marrying the first time – not because my first husband was a bad guy, but because we were so young. We did not have any more business getting married than the man in the moon, as my parents often said. The fact is—my dad made a wrong thing right. I said, "I forgive you, Daddy." It was a beautiful moment. I cry every time I think about it.

There was another situation, one that involved David, where a man came to him and repented for saying something that made David unsure about marrying me. It had caused him a great deal of pain and confusion for a time after our wedding. The man explained that he was simply hurt that David did not marry his daughter and become his son-in-law. Again, we had a chance to forgive and once again to know for sure that we had been obedient when we married.

Those were two significant events that happened in that season following my surrender where the possibility of bitterness cropping up in a later season was cut off. God was clearing a path for us. Even though I was a few years into the journey, I was still just getting started on the road to recovery.

I can look back through the years and see that ever since that season came and went, I have had a much easier time forgiving people when I am wronged. And trust me; I've had a lot of practice. We simply cannot go through this life without being hurt, rejected, misunderstood, or falsely accused. We are also not going to go through this life without hurting people either, whether we mean to or not. So I am sure that you have had many opportunities, or perhaps you currently have opportunity to forgive someone—maybe more than one.

At this level of basic training, I knew very little about how to really let someone go, but at this level of sincerity, I did not need to know very much. I was hungry to know the freedom God had for me. It was a choice of innocence. In childlike humility, I wanted as much as I could get from God. He did not take me through the process like drinking from a waterfall. It was "precept upon precept, line upon line, here a little, there a little" (Isaiah 28:10). He showed me simple truths over and over again and then led me to practice those truths repeatedly until I was ready to move on.

For the Bible Tells Me So

The Scriptures are clear on forgiveness. It is the foundation of the gospel. Jesus died so that we could receive forgiveness of sins. We were born in sin, separated from God and as a result, we continued to walk in sin until we responded to the Coach, who came knocking at our heart's door on behalf of the Father who drew us by His kindness and His love.

There are specific scriptures that tell us to ask for forgiveness as well as to forgive others. Scripture also encourages us to be gracious and patient with those who offend us the same way, over and over again. God knows that if we become weighted down with unforgiveness or a need to be forgiven, it can prohibit us from being successful as we move toward our destiny. It robs us of our joy, and it is toxic to our health over time. There is nothing finer in this life than living in relationships with nothing to prove and nothing to hide. It is so liberating that you can get to the place where you would go out of your way to make offenses right. It is just not worth holding on to anything! We must strive to settle our accounts as quickly as possible and do it with the right motivation and in love.

Forgiving Others

> For if you forgive others their trespasses, your heavenly Father will also forgive you, but if you do not forgive others their trespasses, neither will your Father forgive your trespasses (Matthew 6:14-15).

There is nothing worse than getting cross with the Father while you are hanging on to your offenses. In a later season of my life, I was struggling with forgiving someone. The longer I held on to the offense, the harder it became for me to pray. I had a green chair, circa 1972. It was my prayer chair. I knelt there to pray every day. It suddenly became hard for me to go to my chair to pray. I began to get busy and avoid the chair. However, I began to miss my fellowship with the Father. One morning, as I was passing by the room where my prayer chair was located, as I glanced at it, I asked the Father why it was so hard for me to go there. He said, "There can only be one King on the throne, and that is Me. When you try to be king over your own life, we become like two magnets that repel one another. This is why you find it difficult to approach the chair. At this point, you must surrender your throne for Mine." So I did. I also chose to forgive the person with whom I was struggling to forgive and the Father helped me through the process. First Peter 5:5b exhorts us, "Clothe yourselves, all of you, with humility toward one another, for 'God opposes the proud but gives grace to the humble.'"

> Put on then, as God's chosen ones, holy and beloved, compassionate hearts, kindness, humility, meekness, and patience, bearing with one another and, if one has a complaint against another, forgiving each other; as the Lord has forgiven you, so you also must forgive (Colossians 3:12-13).

I have heard it said that, "In the Kingdom of God, we must be professional forgivers." This is so true! We are examples that others should be able to look to for moral integrity and a life of peace that is so attractive they want it at any cost. In a world that is growing in fear and anxiety, we need to be at peace with all men (Romans 12:18) and be ready to show others how to do the same.

> Then his master summoned him and said to him, 'You wicked servant! I forgave you all that debt because you pleaded with me. And should not you have had mercy on your fellow servant, as I had mercy on you?' And in anger his master delivered him to the jailers, until he should pay all his debt (Matthew 18:32-34).

Jesus' parable about the unforgiving servant illustrates the prison we must endure until we are ready to face our unforgiveness and let it go. The Master in this story forgave a huge debit (signifying the debt of sin that Christ paid for us). In turn, however, the servant who was forgiven refused to forgive a much smaller debt, by comparison. The Master was angry and turned that wicked servant over to the jailer (some translations say tormentor). He was tortured until he paid back the debt he was forgiven prior to his unforgiveness. His end shows us the gravity of our unforgiveness – to lose what had already once been forgiven by the Master, or in reality, the Father. Do not allow yourself to hang out in the enemy's prison cell. Find forgiveness quickly. Then maintain your freedom by making things right as soon as offenses come.

> Then Peter came up and said to him, 'Lord, how often will my brother sin against me, and I forgive him? As many as seven times?' Jesus said to him, 'I do not say to you seven times, but seventy-seven times' (Matthew 18:21-22).

Forgiveness and trust are not the same. The writer of Proverbs said, "As a dog returns to his vomit, so a fool returns to his folly." If someone is hurting you consistently and wants to revisit that sin again and again, you do not have to be a party to it, especially if the sin is self-destructive or is abusive to you or your family. Even Jesus told his disciples in Matthew 10:23a, "When they persecute you in one town, flee to the next." Forgive your offenders consistently, but set boundaries for those who continue to commit the same destructive offense over and over again. Pray for them fervently, and trust them only as they respond to the conviction of the Holy Spirit and exhibit true repentance. Then they can be reconciled back into a healthy relationship. If at some point they fall into this same destructive cycle, put the boundaries back in place until true repentance occurs again. Some habits are difficult to break. Consistency with boundaries will keep you from falling into co-dependent habits of your own as you are standing your ground with a loved one who struggles with habitually harmful behavior.

Keeping records can be stressful. I keep up with multiple bank accounts as I run our family finances as well as that of several companies. I have to reconcile my accounts regularly to maintain integrity in matters of finance. It is stressful and sometimes, if I am not diligent, I may miss something that could cost me service fees, and I become overwhelmed. Likewise, when we try to keep too many accounts of the people who have offended us, we can incur the spiritual consequences of unforgiveness, which can easily turn to bitterness.

"If your brother sins against you, go and tell him his fault, between you and him alone. If he listens to you, you have gained your brother" (Matthew 18:15).

"Be on your guard! If your brother sins, rebuke him; and if he repents, forgive him" (Luke 17:3).

When people do things that hurt you, tell them. You can be kind in so doing. If the person who hurt you apologizes, forgive. In fact, verbalize that forgiveness, and it will bless them and keep your relationship healthy.

Trust God with the burdens of those who might hurt or offend you in some way, tomorrow or next week. It is difficult to go through this life without making a few mistakes and hurting others in the process. It is a part of failing forward. That is fine, as long as we all repent when we hurt someone and forgive when someone hurts us. Deal only with the worries of today, and do not hold on to the past or anticipate what will happen tomorrow. Remain free in your heart and mind by refusing to keep records of wrongs (1 Corinthians 13:5d).

Asking for Forgiveness

Keeping forgiveness at the forefront of our daily lives is commanded in Scripture. Repentance and forgiveness should be like breathing to us. There is not a day that should ever pass but what we worship the Lord in Spirit and in truth. The Scriptures tell us that we cannot even do this until we are sure that we have no one to forgive and no one from whom to be forgiven.

Matthew 5:23 states,

> Therefore, if you are offering your gift at the altar and there remember that your brother or sister has something against you, leave your gift there in front of the altar. First go and be reconciled to them; then come and offer your gift.

When you ask someone for forgiveness, be specific. Do not use words like, "I am sorry that you feel that way." Specify what you did to hurt the person you hurt or even what they perceived that you did when you ask for forgiveness. It is important accountability for you and very important in the offended to know that you are genuine and to genuinely forgive you.

Forgiving Yourself

> "Therefore humble yourselves under the mighty hand of God, that He may exalt you at the proper time, casting all your anxiety on Him, because He cares for you. Be of sober spirit, be on the alert. Your adversary, the devil,

prowls around like a roaring lion, seeking someone to devour" (1 Peter 5:6-8).

As I counsel, I frequently find that the residual struggle of forgiveness in people's lives usually has to do with forgiving themselves. This seems to be the most difficult level of forgiveness. Not only is the devil beating us up for what we may have done, but we are usually pretty good at agreeing with him and throwing in some of our own condemnation for good measure!

It is time to stop laboring over what you did, why you did it, how you did it, and so on. Just admit your part in whatever happened. While you are at it, you probably need to also confess that you have been holding on to this for too long. Search yourself to see if you have fallen into self-hatred as well. These are all things for which you need to repent.

People come into my office and tell me some of the most tragic stories I have ever heard, details of great pain and suffering. I am always amazed at how well the enemy has done to others the same as he has done to me and in many cases, much worse. However, I always bring them back around to the same point. The god of this world is working hard to kill, steal, and destroy before his time is up. He wanted to take their destiny out in the process as well. Jesus knew this was going to happen to them, and the cross was the provision for every tragedy that would ever happen in this life. We must never forget that!

You will have an opportunity at the end of this chapter to use a tool that will help you forgive yourself as well as others.

Forgiving God

God has stated in His Word how much He dislikes murmuring, grumbling, and complaining (Numbers 14:27, Philippians 2:14). These behaviors do not work if you are trying to get God's attention! Persistent faith must be laced with gratitude.

Sometimes when things do not go exactly as we think they should, we get offended at God for, seemingly, not doing His part. This is an error in judgment, based on a lack of knowledge of His character as well as all of the facts that only He can see. We do not always know all of the circumstances. Sometimes we do not have enough scriptural insight to make a judgment call. To lay charge against the Maker of the Universe is highly presumptuous, and yet we feel what we feel. He knows this.

There is a Biblical protocol for asking for God's help, which we must remember. If you are complaining, grumbling, and murmuring as you petition God in prayer, do not expect much. If He commands us not to do this, why would we expect Him to listen to it in prayer? How we ask for God's help matters. Plenty of Scriptures can guide us to pray in faith, taking authority over the enemy (which a lot of people do not do in prayer), thanking God for His help, and resting in the outcome. (Matthew 6:9, Matthew 4, James 1:5-6, 4:10, Luke 10:19, Philippians 4:6-7).

Yet, confessing your anger at God for allowing things to happen in your life or those you love may be helpful. It is how you confess it that counts. Words are important and carry with them life and death (Proverbs 18:21). What you say is not as important as how you say it. This is true in any context and not just in prayer. People tend to respond to how carefully you say things rather than react to hearing you say everything you are thinking, especially in the heat of frustration. Just because you feel like it, you do not get to give people a piece of your mind. In the end, we will give an account for the words we have spoken carelessly. Matthew 12:36-37, Jesus stated, "I tell you, on the day of judgment people will give account for every careless word they speak, for by your words you will be justified, and by your words you will be condemned." The worksheet at the end of this chapter, should you choose to use it, will show you how to simply articulate what event(s) that you believe harmed you, how they made you feel, and what they told you about your identity. God already knows how you feel inside and He has truth to reveal to you in regard to those events: truth that will set you free! Our hearts change when someone explains things about an event that we did not know or that we may have misunderstood. In the same way, confessing how you feel that God let you down gives Him an opportunity to show you the truth in regard to those disappointments as well.

"Be anxious for nothing, but in everything by prayer and supplication with thanksgiving let your requests be made known to God. And the peace of God, which surpasses all comprehension, will guard your hearts and your minds in Christ Jesus. Finally, brethren, whatever is true, whatever is honorable, whatever is right, whatever is pure, whatever is lovely, whatever is of good repute, if there is any excellence and if anything worthy of praise, dwell on these things" (Phillipians 4:6-8).

We need to move along and take care of business before this unforgiveness gets out of hand. Take a look below at the progression of unforgiveness. This stuff is dangerous!

Unforgiveness Leads to Murder!

Refusing to let go of unforgiveness can cause us to develop a strong sense of entitlement. Sometimes our refusal to let it go is so that we do not have to give up the entitlement. Here is a great illustration of why it is so important to let go of unforgiveness as the progression of unforgivness leads all the way to murder.

<u>Unforgiveness</u>
"I am not willing to forgive and I will always remember what they did to me."

<u>Resentment</u>
Feeling ill will, thinking, "I do not like them. I will never forgive them." This keeps unforgiveness in place.

<u>Retaliation</u>
"They should pay for what they did", a decision to think about getting even.

Anger & Wrath
Once retaliation becomes strong enough, plans begin to formulate of how to hurt the perpetrator. Hatred–"They deserve to pay for what they did"; now looking for opportunities to execute vengeance toward the perpetrator.

Violence
Anger and hatred in action; striking, throwing things, screaming, or abuse of some kind will take form in a moment of emotional outburst.

Murder
Either actual murder through abuse gone too far, premeditated murder, or character assassination through gossip, slander, extreme repetitive emotional and verbal abuse.[3]

Guess which sin the enemy is using as a door of access to the minds of people so that he is able to get them to carry out his highest level of evil deeds? You guessed it! Unforgiveness is the sin that leads to murder!

Finally, unforgiveness is a sin unto death. It makes us sick if we do not let it go. Taken too far, it could lead us to an early grave. Some researchers suggest that emotions like anger and resentment cause stress hormones to accumulate in the blood, and that forgiveness reduces this build up.[4]

In a CNN Health report, Senior Medical Correspondent Elizabeth Cohen writes, "Feeling bitter interferes with the body's hormonal and immune systems, according to Carsten Wrosch, an associate professor of psychology at Concordia University in Montreal and an author of a chapter in the new book (*Embitterment: Societal, psychological, and clinical perspectives*). Studies have shown that bitter, angry people have higher blood pressure and heart rate and are more likely to die of heart disease and other illnesses."[5]

Now that we have thoroughly discussed the subject of forgiveness, would you like to take a shot at the forgiveness worksheet that follows? This would be a great way for you to release people from the last chapter's application exercise, but it will also take you a "step beyond forgiveness" so that you can find peace and have a sweet encounter with the Lord.

How to Forgive

Right now, if you are struggling with unforgiveness, and as you decide to use the worksheet at the end of this chapter, you need to see your tragedy swallowed up in Christ's tragedy. You can take your struggles and prayerfully nail them to the cross where His victory swallowed up everything that has ever happened to you. Understand that you are going to be victorious over this because Jesus has already been touched with your pain, your sin, and your infirmities, and took them all with Him to the cross! Today can be your day of freedom from this self-imposed prison.

Before you turn the page to the forgiveness worksheet, let me give you some instruction that may help you. God designed you with all the right physical and spiritual equipment to have fellowship with Him. He has given you "spiritual ears" to hear His voice (John 10:27). He gave you a beautiful mind with an imagination that He designed just for dreams and visions so that you could "see" what He is trying to "say" to you (Joel 2:28-29; Acts 2:17-18). Seeing and hearing something reinforces the truth we are trying to absorb. Inviting the Lord into the areas of your deepest need and residual pain is such a blessing, and He has given us all we need to have this experience. Remember, without faith, it is impossible to please God. "For whoever would draw near to God must believe that HE IS" [Emphasis mine]. He is real and He really wants to speak to you in this forgiveness exercise. So open your heart and let Him do it.

The prophet Joel said that in the last days, God was going to pour out His spirit upon all flesh – that includes you! He said that He would give dreams, visions, and His Spirit to communicate to us just as we communicate to Him. Later, in Acts 2:17 and following, Peter confirms that on the Day of Pentecost, this prophecy was fulfilled. He did it then, and He continues to it today. So you have all the equipment you need to hear, see, and sense His presence and activity in your life. So, "taste and see that the Lord is good! Blessed is the man who takes refuge in Him" (Psalm 34:8).

As we seek Him for the grace to forgive, doesn't a refuge sound inviting? I hope you think so.

The following forgiveness worksheet has all the instructions on it that you will need to forgive others, yourself, and God completely. Finish it all the way to the end. I dare you! Use it as a tool now and in the future not only to keep you in a place of forgiveness, but also to identify lies about your identity to which the Lord wants to speak His truth. Learn to use empathy to help you release difficult people, and finally practice taking authority over the enemy and speaking blessing over your life! You can do this!

In Closing

Father, I pray in the beautiful Name of Jesus, that You would bless the readers, right now, with Your amazing grace, should they choose to take Your hand and walk together with You through this forgiveness worksheet. You are mighty to save, heal, and deliver, and You have the words of life that will redeem every event and heal every hurt. I consecrate these precious ones into Your capable hands Abba. I bind the voice of the enemy and ask for "red carpet" access into Your throne room for this ministry time they are about to undertake. You are good and Your love endures forever. Please enfold them with that powerful love as they seek to release unforgiveness from their lives and health. I thank You for what You desire to do in Your children and that You are faithful to perform it to the praise and glory of the Son, who makes this all possible! I give you thanks again. Amen.

Chapter Seven

Personal Application

1. The Holy Spirit is also the Spirit of

_____

2. Write out the Scripture that impacted you the most for each area of forgiveness covered in this chapter.
a) Forgiving others

_____

_____

b) Asking for forgiveness

_____

c) Forgiving yourself

_____

d) Forgiving God

_____

4. In the progression of unforgiveness, how far have you let yourself go before you found it in your heart to forgive someone? How did this affect your health?

_____

_____

Would you like to use the forgiveness tool today to work through some issues of unforgiveness in your own life? If so, follow the instructions on the forgiveness ministry worksheet and know that the Father is waiting for you, and the Holy Spirit will take it from here.

FORGIVENESS MINISTRY WORKSHEET

Step 1: **Write down the name of the persons you want to forgive below.** (After the instructions and examples, you have spaces on this worksheet to work through 5 things for which you need to forgive the person(s). There are also 2 spaces to work on forgiving yourself and God, if necessary.

PERSON(s) I WANT TO FORGIVE TODAY (Put the names of the persons you need to forgive here):

_____

Step 2: In the spaces that follow these instructions, write down each person's name and how they hurt you in each of the first blanks.

EXAMPLE:
A) <u>Dad</u> , you hurt me when <u>you abandoned me when I was six years old.</u>

Step 3: Ponder a moment and ask God to help you describe how this made you feel when the person hurt you.

EXAMPLE:
You made me feel <u>very sad. I felt very alone. I also felt like there was no one there to protect me. I was very embarrassed</u>

<u>when people asked me questions about my Dad and I had to tell them what you did.</u>

Step 4: Now, go a little deeper and think about how it made you feel about YOURSELF. That will come in the form of an "I am _____" or "I was _____" statement (see example below). These are core lies we want to offer up to God in exchange for the truth ourselves.

EXAMPLE:
And that made me feel like <u>I was not loveable or unworthy to be loved.</u>

John 10:27 says that if we have a relationship with Jesus, we are His sheep, and we will hear His voice. Furthermore, in Acts 2, when the Holy Spirit was poured out and the church was born, that event fulfilled a prophecy from Joel 2 which says that "in the last days" God would pour out His spirit on "all flesh," and that they would be given prophetic sight through dreams and visions, where God would reveal Himself and speak to them. Jeremiah 33:3 also says, "Call to me and I will answer you and I will show you great and mighty things that you do not know."

Step 5: Pray the following prayer for each event. Ask God to show you His truth about the lie-based pain you have just identified.

"Father, I choose to forgive [person you are forgiving] **for** [what they did to you] **because it made me feel** [how it made you feel]**. Search my heart and show me your truth. What is the truth you want me to know Lord?"** **(Close your eyes, listen and watch, then write down what you see or hear or sense coming from the Lord, whether it is a Scripture, a picture, something He says, etc.)**

Write down the truth God shows you in the last line of each section.

EXAMPLE:
The truth God is showing me is <u>I was always loveable because I was destined to choose Him and become His child. I was also loveable because I was created in God's image. I can see Jesus standing by my bed at night watching over my life as I grew, waiting for the day that I would come to know Him.</u>

MINISTRY WORKSHEET

1) _____, you hurt me when you _____

_____

_____

_____

You made me feel

_____

_____

_____

And that made me feel like I

_____

_____

_____

(Pray the prayer Here. Watch and listen for the Lord's truth).

Forgiveness Ministry Worksheet

The truth God is showing me is

_____

_____

_____

2) _____, you hurt me when you _____

_____

_____

_____

You made me feel

_____

_____

And that made me feel like I

_____

_____

(Pray the prayer Here. Watch and listen for the Lord's truth).

The truth God is showing me is

_____

_____

_____

3) _____, you hurt me when you _____

_____

_____

_____

You made me feel

_____

_____

_____

And that made me feel like I

_____

_____

_____

(Pray the prayer Here. Watch and listen for the Lord's truth).
The truth God is showing me is

_____

_____

_____

4) _____, you hurt me when you _____

_____

_____

_____

Forgiveness Ministry Worksheet

You made me feel

_____

_____

_____

And that made me feel like I

_____

_____

_____

(Pray the prayer Here. Watch and listen for the Lord's truth).
The truth God is showing me is

_____

_____

_____

5) _____, you hurt me when you _____

_____

_____

_____

You made me feel

_____

_____

_____

And that made me feel like I

_____

_____

(Pray the prayer Here. Watch and listen for the Lord's truth).
The truth God is showing me is

_____

_____

_____

6) _____, you hurt me when you _____

_____

_____

_____

You made me feel

_____

_____

And that made me feel like I

_____

_____

(Pray the prayer Here. Watch and listen for the Lord's truth).

Forgiveness Ministry Worksheet

The truth God is showing me is

_____

_____

_____

7) _____, you hurt me when you _____

_____

_____

_____

You made me feel

_____

_____

_____

And that made me feel like I

_____

_____

_____

(Pray the prayer Here. Watch and listen for the Lord's truth).

The truth God is showing me is

_____

_____

_____

Understand that we cannot change the past. But the Spirit of God can REDEEM what we believe about what happened to us—which almost always has affected our sense of worth. John 8:32 says, **"Then you will know the truth, and the truth will set you free." Forgiving does not really let the one forgiven off the hook; it really sets you free from the torment of unforgiveness and the havoc it plays on your physical health and mental peace.**

Forgiveness of others and letting go of the past are difficult for this reason. But not letting go of the past can prohibit us from moving on with our lives. OR unforgiveness can suddenly surface, causing us problems in other current relationships or in future relationships.

Step 4: Step Beyond Forgiveness:

Peter was hurt by the same person over and over again, so he asked Jesus, "Lord, how many times must I forgive? Seven times? Jesus replied, "I do not say to you seven times, but seventy-seven times" (Matthew 18:21-22). In saying this, Jesus was speaking of how much he would forgive us when he would die on the cross for our sins, which are many, and often times repeated over and over again.

In the Bible, we see that Job, Stephen, and Jesus all did something similar that was powerful in the realm of forgiveness. They asked God to forgive their offenders. Job's friends could not be healed until Job prayed and asked God to forgive them (Job 42:7-10). Stephen, as an angry mob was stoning him to death said, **"Lord, do not hold this sin against them"** (Acts 7:59-60). Finally, Jesus said as He was hanging on the cross, **"Father, forgive them, for they do not know what they are doing"** (Luke 23:34).

Step 5: Empathy Helps

When you stop to consider that "hurting people hurt people," and as you ask the Lord to help you understand what your offender was going through when he/she hurt you, forgiveness becomes easier. Many times we do not understand why people do what they do in the moments it is happening. However, after years of maturing, we often develop a greater understanding of why our offender made certain choices and the Lord has even more perspective on things that we still may not see very well. Take a moment and ask the Lord to show you beyond what you already understand about your offender's choices and write down what you see from His larger perspective.

_____

_____

_____

_____

_____

_____

_____

_____

_____

_____

_____

_____

_____

_____

In the following prayer, you will be praying the same powerful prayer as Jesus did. In this way, you are letting your offender's off of God's hook as well as your own.

> **Father, I CHOOSE to forgive _____ who has done things that hurt me. I also choose to forgive You for allowing these things to happen in my life. I choose to release them from any charge that is against them for what they did to me. I release them entirely into Your hands. I forgive them because I choose to do so in obedience to Your command. I forgive them because You have already forgiven me.**
>
> **And Father, I recognize the enemy's hand in what was done to me. I ask that YOU would forgive them and release them because hurting people hurt people, they are motivated by the evil one according to your word, and they couldn't have fully known what they were doing to me. Please do not hold their sins against them as I also release them with Your help and by Your strength at work in me. They are free to resolve this from this point forward. And in the Name of Jesus, I am finally free as well. Amen.**

Now pray this final declaration.

> **Lord Jesus, I choose not to hold on to my resentment. I let go of my right to seek revenge and ask You to heal my damaged emotions. Thank You for setting me free from the bondage of my bitterness. I now ask You to bless those who have hurt me. In Jesus' Name I pray. Amen.**

Chapter Eight

GOING TO THE HIGH PLACES
♛

"He made my feet like the feet of a deer and set me secure on the heights. He trains my hands for war, so that my arms can bend a bow of bronze" (Psalm 18:33-34).

I had been immersed in the Word of God for two years by this time. The tension between David and me was diminishing because God was bringing to pass for me His promise in Psalm 107:20: "He sent out His word and healed them; and delivered them from their destruction." The remedial training was coming to an end, and I was becoming strong enough to endure the next season. The Coach knew where we were headed. He knew that I trusted Him enough now that, as we walked into the oncoming storms, I would not let go of His hand.

Something else in me had also changed. One day I woke up and felt an overwhelming desire to have a child. I talked to David about it and, after a while, he also came to faith about trusting God for providing what we would need to start a family.

However, it did not take long to discover that I would not be successful in conceiving a child. Perhaps I had been on birth control for too long. Maybe I still had too much stress in my body. For whatever reason, conceiving a child was not as easy as having the desire, as many of you probably know all too painfully well.

In the spring of 1991, I was fed up! My family always said, "There is more than one way to skin a cat!" That is a terrible colloquialism, but life had trained me that if one thing did not work, try another. So, I remembered how the Word of God spoke about child-like faith, and I decided that I would join forces with those who had a stronger one than mine!

I went to a man who was our children's pastor at the time. I asked him if I could come up to the children's church and have the kids agree with me in prayer for a special need. He agreed to it, and I attended children's church that day.

After the service, I came forward and told the children that Mr. David and I really wanted to have children. As I spoke you could see the faith rising up in them. Their eyes danced with excitement, and their hearts were resolute. I could tell that this was no big thing for these little soldiers. After I spoke, Pastor Jonathan invited them to come forward and lay hands on me and join him in prayer. They came forward and I had little hands everywhere, but I did not care in the least. Even a few of them took turns praying out loud. These children were not taking no for an answer. They prayed and believed God with me, and I received something that day.

By May, David and I were headed to Florida for vacation. I had never felt so happy as I did since the time those kids prayed for me. It was almost as if a gift of faith had been dropped into my spirit. While we were in Florida, I curiously noticed the signs before boarding each ride at Disney World. I still got on, and David and I had the best time together. As the trip was coming to an end, I began to sense that I was pregnant. It was a knowing deep inside me, a confirmation of peace from the Coach.

On the way home, we stopped in Georgia to visit friends for a few days. I told my friend that I thought I was pregnant, so she excitedly grabbed her purse and ran to the store to get a pregnancy test for me. I took the test and sure enough, it was positive!

I waited until we were on the road before I told David about the test. He was completely blindsided by the news. I think he had somehow prepared his mind so completely for the worst – that we would not get pregnant – that he was shocked! He said, "You cannot know for sure. What if that test is wrong?"

I said, "I am pregnant David. I knew it before I took the test." He did not believe me for a minute. So we decided that we would discuss it no further until I could get confirmation from a doctor.

On the way home, however, a familiar sense of foreboding was settling in on me. It was that same old spirit of fear. I began to think about the twins. Although I was certain they were in good hands with the Lord, I could not help but think about their premature death. Why did it happen? What if it happened again? I never said anything to David until we were home. We talked about it. He was compassionate towards me and prayed that if, indeed, I was pregnant, that the Lord would preserve and protect our child.

As I waited for my scheduled appointment, I decided to go and see a man I only knew as an acquaintance in the city. At the time, Cliff Sharp was the director over what was known at the time as the Crisis Pregnancy Center. I was not sure why I was going to see him other than the fact that I felt a strong nudge of the Holy Spirit to go. My sensitivity to the Coach was growing, and it boosted my confidence in Him.

I dropped by the clinic and asked to see Mr. Sharp. He was the kindest, most precious man. As I sat there talking to him, I wondered at how his compassion was such a blessing for this type of ministry. I told him that I thought I was pregnant, but that David was still a bit in denial. So he said, "Well let's find out, shall we?" He handed me a pregnancy test and once again, it was positive! After he congratulated me, I began to tell him about how I lost the twins and about how that fear of loss was trying to creep back in on me; that I was afraid for this child as well. He asked if I wanted to agree with him in prayer. I gladly accepted. We joined hands, and this man prayed the most powerful, most precious prayer over me and my child.

I will never forget that day. He bound the spirit of fear and asked the Lord to hold back the forces of the enemy who may attempt to threaten the life of this child. There was so much more to his prayer, and I left feeling settled in my spirit.

The day came when David accompanied me to the doctor. The blood test revealed that indeed, we were going to have a baby! Finally, David allowed himself to be happy. He was relieved to have conclusive proof. I am certain he was also a bit nervous to finally own the responsibility of becoming a first-time father. We talked again about the powerful prayer that Mr. Sharp prayed over me. It was only a few days later that, after his morning devotions, David came to me and said that he felt the Lord direct him to lay hands on my belly every day and declare a blessing of health, peace, safety, and life over our child. And so we did.

Honestly, in all of my life, I do not remember happier days than when I carried this child. I have never felt more beautiful. Carrying life inside of me and knowing that my body was its protection was the most incredible feeling in the world. I sang to this child. I read to this child. I prayed for this child. I talked to this child. And then the day came when we would know if this new addition was going to be a girl or a boy!

David once again accompanied me to the doctor. As I lay in the ultrasound exam room, the familiar feeling of a cold transducer gliding across my slick belly, I would not have been at all surprised if I had twins because I seemed to be bigger than normal for twenty weeks. However, there was only one child, and it was a little girl. I remember it like it was yesterday. Something came over David Robertson like I had never seen. This child was suddenly REAL, and she had to have a name from that point forward. We called her Abigail Grace Robertson. She would be a "Joy of the Father," and He would bring this little blessing forth by His grace.

I remember the day when I prayed and said, "Lord, I have never known a love as powerful as the one I feel for this baby. Carrying her has been the greatest joy of my life so far. But I am afraid that if you do not change my heart, I am content to carry her until you come." I have since met a few other women who felt the same.

It would only be a few more months, and just prior to her due date, when I contracted pneumonia. I became so ill that I was miserable. I was ready to have this baby! It was just weeks before her birth was imminent. I was facing the dawn of the next season of my life. God had this planned from the beginning, I am sure. Jesus was ready to do His part. The Coach was about to take my hand and walk me into the biggest storm of my life. The season of redemption was about to dawn. Basic Combat Training boot camp was about to begin.

In Summary

As children, our knowledge comes through our families of origin, our circles of influence, what we hear, what we witness, our education, spiritual guidance (The Bible or whatever religious guidance is used), and what we learn from personal experience. Most of my spiritual knowledge came from what I heard in church services, in Sunday school Bible stories, and what I sang in children's choir. The only thing I really knew about the devil, for years, is that if he did not like what Jesus was doing, he could sit on a tack—until I saw a demon manifest in a human being. This was hardly something to flippantly tell to, "Go sit on it."

But I also saw the evidence of the Holy Spirit come into a room and miraculously heal people. I watched as limbs grew out. I saw an evangelist hit a huge lump on a woman's back and it disappear! I watched people get up out of wheelchairs and walk! I saw the evidence of the Holy Spirit sit down UPON people, and they danced all over the room with their eyes shut. I heard them being baptized in the Holy Spirit as they yielded to the gift of tongues. I literally watched a woman fall out under the overwhelming power of the Spirit. She was standing next to a large communion table and her head was too close. She was going to hit that table right around her neck. I remember how I gasped as she was falling when suddenly it looked like she fell right THROUGH the communion table. Her body did not bend, nor did she hit the table. But when she landed, she was under the table! I was blinking and weeping and flinching in disbelief. She was better than fine when she got up! It was a powerful environment in which to grow up, and I am thankful for my spiritual heritage because, as you have already seen, the day came when I would need that power for myself—and He came. Yet, darkness did not relent.

It was something that, for years, I could not explain. Caught in the fray of a fierce battle over my life, with all of the doubt and fear that plagued my mind, if someone would have ever asked me what it was like to be a Christian, it would have been difficult to explain my life. I did not know what I had done so wrong that the devil could overtake me so easily. I was still lacking knowledge about spiritual warfare: about how our lives can have open doors to the enemy, and how to use authority over the enemy in my prayer life, and so on. However, the season of training was just around the corner, where the enemy would, once again, contend for my life—several times.

It would take forty-five years for the healing love of God to reach the core of my fear. I had to begin basic training long before that time. In the words of Joyce Meyer, I had to face the fear and, "Do it afraid!"[1] The subsequent shell I built around my inner man was thick and tough. I was like an artichoke. I had to be peeled all the way down to the heart before I found the fullness of my freedom. It makes me weep when I think about how long it took me to get completely free. You will be reading book three in this series before this happens. The good news is that, with the years of experience finding freedom, I am able to help others find it much quicker and easier.

Although it makes me weep to think about how long it took me to get free, it makes me weep for joy when I think back at how good God has been to me for a very long time. He has redeemed my life from the destructive force of hell, He has trained my hands for battle, and I am alive to tell of His goodness, and to teach, train, and help others.

Just out of curiosity, when I began to write this book, I asked my Dad this question: "Daddy, why do you think I had all of those near-death experiences and was tormented for so long?"

Without hesitation, he answered, "It was because the enemy was trying to kill you, Baby. Somehow he knew what God had planned for your life." I would add that God used the suffering to give me greater compassion for others going through tests and trials and to fashion understanding, skill, and intuition as a counselor. This is clearer to us now, but it took quite a few years to connect the dots and to understand it fully.

What Have We Learned?

In this first book of the series, I hope that you have been able to identify, through my story, how the enemy begins his work early in our lives. He wants to undermine our faith as soon as possible using the circumstances of life as the framework to weave a deceptive web of lies about our identity, our security, God's goodness, and God's plan for our lives. He wants to keep sin patterns in operation as far down the generational line as possible. Finally, he wants to keep us so angry and in disunity with family and others that we never let go of unforgiveness and bitterness. Hopefully, you have found the ministry worksheets to help you with some of these instances in your own life. The concepts illustrated in the tools are something you can use over and over again in your walk with Christ. Use them until you learn to identify lies in the moment, offer them to the Lord and receive truth from the Word or from His voice. Use them to help you develop your prayer life until you learn to not only repent but to renounce the enemy and take authority over his schemes to control your life.

If you would like additional copies of the worksheets, you may obtain them at www.thewaylady.com, under "More" and "Free Resources."

I hope you have noticed how much God the Holy Spirit, our Kingdom Coach, becomes involved in our lives, particularly after salvation. He is always available to us, even though we do not always know or believe the truth about His availability. In fact, He has promised never to leave and never to forsake us (Hebrews 13:5). Until we are instructed by the Word of God, we are unable to walk in obedience to what it says. We may not resolve the incapacity to receive God's love. We may not see His promises fulfilled because of disobedience. It takes the Word to illuminate these truths to our hearts and minds and to activate our faith in His promises. Until then, however, He is still using everything that happens to us to draw us closer and to train us for the future. He is working all things together for our good (Romans 8:28).

Through our ignorance and lack of obedience, the enemy may still have access to our circumstances. As we fail to consider his involvement, it appears that God is not being fair or keeping His Word. However, if we stay on the path with God and, at some point, begin to walk closer with Him (by reading and studying His Word, increased time with Him, inquiring of Him and acknowledging Him), we will discover that He is exactly Whom He claims to be and does everything He promised.

If you have been saved for any time at all, but little in your life has changed—whether your behavior or your circumstances—I encourage you to keep reading this series and to consider taking a step up in your relationship with God.

My parents and I have walked together through the years of my adult life. They have seen how the Lord has taken what the enemy meant for my destruction and turned it around for my good and the good of many others. This is God's redemptive plan for all of us! He wants to take our wounds, our struggles, and our fears and fashion them into compassion to comfort others the same way we have been comforted by Him (2 Corinthians 1:4). God wants to redeem every minute of pain and turn our suffering into perseverance and reverent submission: clothing us with power and bringing us under His protection. Nothing is wasted in God's economy. This plan is so important because of the days in which we are living. The days ahead will demand a line of demarcation to be drawn between those who will make the Kingdom of God their priority (which will require them to be living in freedom and experiencing joy in the midst of a world that is unraveling), and those who will continue and fall even deeper into fear, anxiety, and chaos.

One final exhortation: Go after your healing without delay. Take your eyes off of yourself, and off of others and get them on Jesus. Your sin is no longer an issue. Offer everyone grace and the benefit of the doubt. Pray, listen, and obey. Live in your Bible. Sing and laugh as much as you can. Be at peace with everyone. Pick your battles wisely. We cannot afford to become ensnared with anything in the days ahead.

Hopefully, you have already seen God's faithfulness in my stories. But there is more—abundantly more that happened once I accepted this special invitation to join the Coach on this next adventure. It had a bumpy start, but it became the adventure of a lifetime! I hope to share those stories and more with you as you join me again in the next book of the series, *The Kingdom Coach: Basic Combat Training*.

In Closing

Papa, as I write this final prayer, I want to thank You for pouring this book through me, to share with those You have called to read it. You are an amazing Provider and incredibly good, that my soul knows very well! You are the best coach, Holy Spirit: better than I could have ever dreamed! I am thankful that I finally found a place of stillness with You. It is almost difficult to look back and find myself as who I used to be. You have done so much. I am forever grateful.

Now Lord, would you bless the readers who have remained with me to the end of this first leg of *The Kingdom Coach* journey? Would You also connect the dots for them? As they ponder these stories and spiritual principles again and again, help them to see Your involvement in their own journey to freedom and to the specific calling You have placed on their lives. Show them where You were, what You were doing along the way, and what You would have said could they have heard Your voice.

Engrave the truths that are most applicable to them in the depths of their hearts. May those truths lead them into deeper depths and higher heights with You as they seek to advance the Kingdom in their specific call to ministry. We do not need a pulpit to minister, Lord. Make us fruitful in the areas where You have placed us. May these stories inspire them to receive any remedial training necessary to get them ready for their own adventure! I have no doubt You are already speaking to them about it. Give them ears to hear what You are saying Lord.

Your Kingdom come! Your will be done in the lives of the readers, concerning their lives, their families, their vocations, and their passions; as it is in heaven, so let it be released into the earth. Let them see it coming to pass, my Lord King. Let it be a praise to Your glory. Make them a praise to Your glory.

Put a hunger in their hearts to join us again in the next book. I love You Lord. Cover my readers with your grace, mercy, and Divine favor. Thank You Father. I ask these things in the Name of Your beautiful Son. Amen!

Blessings and peace to you all! See you in the next book!

The WAYLady
www.thewaylady.com

Chapter Eight

Personal Application

1. In addition to any remedial training you listed as needing in practical areas of your life at the beginning of this study, do you see the need for remedial training in the Word of God before you proceed into a new season of your own? Yes   No

2. If you answered "yes" to the above question, what is your plan?

_____

_____

3. Overall, what connections with your own life experiences were you able to make while reading this first book in the Kingdom Coach series?

_____

_____

4. How has reading this book impacted the way you look at spiritual warfare?

_____

5. Write out a prayer of appreciation of your own in regard to the way you have seen God's intervention in your life.

_____

_____

_____

APPENDIX

Statistics on the Bible in America

I researched to see what 2014 polls were saying about the Bible in America. Here is what I found:

According to a study, *"The Bible in American Life,"*[3] conducted by the Center for the Study of Religion and American Culture, 50% of Americans read some form of scripture in the past year, and 48% of those read the Bible. Four in 5 read it at least once a month, and 9% of Americans say they read the Bible daily.

Feelings About the Bible

In the past year, have you read the Bible outside of a worship service?	Inerrant Word of God	Inspired Word of God	Book of Fables	Other
Yes	45%	46%	9%	1%
No	15%	50%	33%	2%

According to the General Social Survey, the report says, nearly eight in ten Americans regard the Bible as either the literal word of God or as inspired by God. Fifty percent of those who have not read the Bible still believe it to be the "divinely inspired Word of God," which is even higher—by 4 percentage points—than those who do read the Bible.

When asked why they read the Bible, respondents named the number one reason as being personal prayer and devotion. Many also said they read the Bible to learn more about their religion—over 78% of Americans identify as Christian, according to Pew Research. Some also read the Bible in search of guidance in personal decisions and improving relationships.

Consulting Scripture for personal prayer is three times more common than turning to the Bible to learn about hot-button issues like abortion, homosexuality, war or poverty. Nearly half of the 48% who do read the Bible on their own said they turned most favorably to the Book of Psalms, particularly noting Psalm 23, which begins "the Lord is my shepherd."[1]

Otherwise, Barna's Research reports...

"1. Bible skepticism is now 'tied' with Bible engagement

This year's research reveals that skepticism toward the Bible continues to rise. For the first time since tracking began, Bible skepticism is tied with Bible engagement. The number of those who are skeptical or agnostic toward the Bible—who believe that the Bible is "just another book of teachings written by men that contains stories and advice"—has nearly doubled from 10% to 19% in just three years. This is now equal to the number of people who are Bible engaged—who read the Bible at least four times a week and believe it is the actual or inspired Word of God.

Digging into the population segmentation of Bible skeptics, we find that two-thirds are 48 or younger (28% Millennials, 36% Gen-Xers), and they are twice as likely to be male (68%) than female (32%). They are more likely to identify as Catholic than any other single denomination or affiliation (30%) and are the most-likely segment not to have attended church (87%) or prayed (63%) during the previous week. They are also most likely not to have made a commitment to Jesus that is important in their life today (76%).

Not only are Millennials more likely to be skeptical toward Scripture, they are also less likely to read the Bible (39% say *they never read the Bible, compared to 26% of all adults), less likely to own a Bible (80% compared to 88%) and less likely to believe the Bible contains everything a person needs to know to live a meaningful life (35% compared to 50%). Given the increase in Millennials who don't believe the Bible is sacred and the decrease in Bible awareness among Millennials, Bible skepticism will likely continue to rise in the next five years.*

2. Despite the declines, most Americans continue to be "pro-Bible."

While the percentage of Americans who believe the Bible is sacred has fallen in recent years, from 86% in 2011 to 79% in 2014, it's still a sizable majority of all adults. In general, Americans continue to view the Bible very positively. More than half of Americans (56%) are "pro-Bible"—meaning they believe the Bible is the actual or inspired word of God with no errors. Most adults say the Bible encourages forgiveness (91%), generosity (88%) and patience (89%) while discouraging war (62%), slavery (60%) and prostitution (82%). Nearly nine in 10 households own at least one Bible (88%) and the average number of Bibles per household is 4.7.

Being pro-Bible doesn't necessarily mean Americans use the Bible regularly, however. Only 37% of Americans report reading the Bible once a week or more. Among those who have read Scripture in the previous week, not quite six in 10 (57%) say they gave a lot of thought to how it might apply to their life. While the Bible's place in America as a cultural icon endures, it's not always perceived as a transformational text. Even as Bible ownership remains strong, readership and engagement are weak."

3. Distraction and busyness continue to squeeze out the Bible.

So what keeps people from reading the Bible they own? Like all other forms of analog media, the Bible is pushed to the side in part because people are just too busy. Among those who say their Bible reading decreased in the last year, the number-one reason was busyness: 40% report being too busy with life's responsibilities (job, family, etc.), an increase of seven points from just one year ago.

Other factors Americans cite as reasons for less time reading Scripture include a significant change in their life (17%), becoming atheist or agnostic (15%), going through a difficult experience that caused them to doubt God (13%) and seeing that reading the Bible made very little difference in someone else's life (8%).[2]

BIBLIOGRAPHY

INTRODUCTION
1. Summer of Monuments. (2014). Wikipedia. Retrieved from http://en.wikipedia.org/wiki/Compassion

2. Ibid

3. Diamond, Stephen, Ph.D. (2012) Evil Deeds. Retrieved from http://www.psychologytoday.com/blog/evil-deeds/201204/essential-secrets-psychotherapy-what-is-the-shadow

4. Remedial. (2014). Merriam-Webster Dictionary. Retrieved from http://www.merriam-webster.com/ dictionary/remedial

CHAPTER ONE: Do We Need Help?
1. Hebrews 3:12. Gills Exposition of the Entire Bible. (2004-2014). Retrieved from http://biblehub.com/hebrews/3-12.htm

2. Romans 12:2. Matthew Henry's Concise Commentary. Biblehub.com. Retrieved from http://biblehub.com/romans/12-2.htm

3. Gurian, A. Ph.D. Early Childhood Development: The First Five Years, Retrieved from http://www.aboutourkids.org/articles/early_childhood_development_first_five_years

4. Child Development and Early Learning. (2008). World Health Organization. Retrieved from http://www.factsforlife-global.org/03/

5. Santrock, J. W. (2012) Essentials of Life-Span Development. New York, NY: McGraw Hill. Pg. 129.

6. Trauma, Attachment, and Stress Disorders: *Rethinking and Reworking Developmental Issues.* Retrieved from http://www.healingresources.info/trauma_attachment_stress_disorders.htm

7. Ibid

CHAPTER TWO: This is My Story

1. Philippians 3:13. Gills Exposition of the Entire Bible. (2004-2014). Biblehub.com. Retrieved from http://biblehub.com/philippians/3-13.htm

2. Genesis 32:24. Matthew Henry's Concise Commentary. (2004-2014). Biblehub.com. Retrieved from http://biblehub.com/commentaries/mhc/genesis/32.htm

3. Vanderlaan, Jennifer. (2014) Labor Challenges. Retrieved from http://www.birthingnaturally.net/birth/challenges/prom.html

4. Skinner, Dr. Kevin B. (2005). Treating Pornography Addiction. Growth Climate, Inc.

CHAPTER THREE: Freedom from Pride and Presumption

1. The Art of Marriage: Getting to the Heart of God's Design. (2011). FamilyLife. Little Rock, AR: FamilyLife Publishing.

CHAPTER FOUR: From Religion to Relationship

1. Larimore, MD, W. and Larimore, B. (2008). His Brain, Her Brain: How Divinely Designed Differences Can Strengthen Your Marriage, Grand Rapids, MI: Zondervan. Pg. 47.

2. Ibid, Pg. 39.

3. Huey, J. (1998) When I Think About the Lord. CFN Music.

CHAPTER FIVE: Freedom from Biblical Illiteracy

1. Hebrews 1:14. Matthew Henry's Concise Commentary. (2004-2014). Biblehub.com. Retrieved from http://biblehub.com/hebrews/1-14.htm

2. Hebrews 1:14. Gill's Exposition of the Entire Bible. (2004-2014). Biblehub.com. Retrieved from http://biblehub.com/hebrews/1-14.htm

3. Chinese Proverb Quotes. (2014). Quotes.net. Retrieved from http://www.quotes.net/quote/9114

4. AboutESVBible.org (2011) Retrieved from http://about.esvbible.org/about/preface/;

Manuscripts used in translating the ESV. Retrieved from https://www.crossway.org/bibles/esv/translation/manuscripts/

5. O'Leary, Amy. (July, 2013). NYTimes.com. Retrieved from http://www.nytimes.com/2013/07/27/technology/the-faithful-embrace-youversion-a-bible-app.html?pagewanted=all&_r=0

6. Bennett, Richard M (1999) Films for Christ. Retrieved from http://christiananswers.net/q-eden/sola-scriptura-bible.html?zoom_highlight=infallibility+of+scripture

7. What is Young's Literal Translation (2002-2014) Got Questions Ministries. Gotquestions.org. Retrieved from http://www.gotquestions.org/Youngs-Literal-Translation-YLT.html#ixzz3ChtvO9Rg

CHAPTER SIX: Freedom from Generational Sins

1. Family Tradition. (2000-2014). AZlyrics.com. Retrieved from http://www.azlyrics.com/lyrics/hankwilliamsjr/familytradition.html

CHAPTER SEVEN: The Freedom of Forgiveness

1. Fowler, James A. (1999) Old Testament Believers and New Testament Christians. Christ in You Ministries, Fall Brook, CA

2. Maxwell, John (2013) Managing The Disciplines of Relationship-Building. Retrieved from http://www.johnmaxwell.com/blog/managing-the-disciplines-of-relationship-building

3. Wright, Henry, Be in Health, Retrieved from http://www.beinhealth.com/public/sites/default/files/Unforgiveness_is_sin_unto_death.pdf

4. Spirituality (2011). Milton S. Hershey Medical Center. Retrieved from http://pennstatehershey.adam.com/content.aspx?productId=107&pid=33&gid=000360

5. Cohen, Elizabeth (2011) Blaming Others Can Ruin Your Health. CNNHealth.com. Retrieved from http://www.cnn.com/2011/HEALTH/08/17/bitter.resentful.ep/

CHAPTER EIGHT: Going to the High Places
1. Meyer, Joyce. (2014) Do It Afraid!

http://www.joycemeyer.org/articles/ea.aspx?article=do_it_afraid

APPENDIX
1. Goff, Phillip, Farnsley, Arther E., Thuesen, Peter J. (March, 2014) The Bible in American Life A National Study by The Center for the Study of Religion and American Culture, Indiana University. Purdue University, Indianapolis, IN

2. Barnagroup (2014) The State of the Bible: 6 Trends for 2014. Retrieved from https://www.barna.org/barna-update/culture/664-the-state-of-the-bible-6-trends-for-2014#.VAk7PmNO18E

CPSIA information can be obtained at www.ICGtesting.com
Printed in the USA
LVOW12s0637281114

415747LV00001B/1/P